MUSICAL COMPOSITION

Projects in Ways and Means

ELLIS B. KOHS

The Scarecrow Press, Inc.
Metuchen, N.J., & London
1980

Musical Calligraphy
by Russ Bartmus

Library of Congress Cataloging in Publication Data

Kohs, Ellis B 1916–
Musical composition.

Bibliography: p.
Includes index.
1. Composition (Music) I. Title.
MT40.K726 781.6′1 79-26990
ISBN 0-8108-1285-1

Preface

Is it possible to teach the *art* of musical composition? This question, though frequently raised, has never been answered with persuasiveness sufficient to put it to rest. Nobody seriously doubts that the use of the tools of basic *craftsmanship* can be taught, provided the student is endowed with intelligence and musical talent, and has the will to pursue musical studies with diligence and an open mind.

But composers are more than skilled craftspeople. They each have a vision of something new, something beyond what they have been taught. It is this vision, this impatience with the status quo, and an intuitive sense as to how one turns dreams into reality, that cannot be taught. Impatience itself does not lead to artistic results: this surging energy must be transformed into a patient search for the technical means of realizing the ends, of materializing the vision.

Sometimes, as with Beethoven or Debussy, the composer appears to be a radical thinker and doer who challenges the precepts regarded by teachers and peers as immutable and beyond question. But not all composers are "radical" in that sense. Some of them (Monteverdi and Ives, for example) are among the first to glimpse the future; one may call these the avant-garde. But others (Mozart is a good example) have by the very perfection of their utterance defined a style, said the last word, and closed a period.

Rarely does one composer belong equally to both categories. Part of the greatness of J. S. Bach lies in his apparent role as father of the modern age, the first to comprehend fully the structural function of tonality; but at the same time, he is the last flowering of the Baroque era—after him nothing further in that style was possible.

Composers may develop their artistry at the same time that they study their craft. Artistry and craftsmanship grow best in a climate of disciplined freedom where teachers and fellow-students have high standards and distant goals, and all have an insatiable appetite for musical knowledge and for music making.

Few truly succeed in this demanding profession. Unfortunately, there are many who aspire to *be*, only to discover—sometimes rather late—that *being* is a far cry from *doing*.

But on the positive side, music is a mansion of many rooms. Many types of creativity are needed in a world that is in the midst of great technological change. The well-trained women or men who are in one of music's many domains should be able to find an appropriate niche for themselves. And the artist-composers, the people of unusual vision, are going to sing their songs, whatever they may be. There is no stopping them.

It is the purpose of this book to go beyond the elements of musicianship, of harmony, form, counterpoint, orchestration, and music history, and to set forth some of the questions related to compositional procedure, style, and esthetics, to help students discover for themselves how to secure and how to judge the best answers. It is aimed at both students and teachers, in the hope that it may serve the needs of both.

The greatest composition teachers, of course, are the great composers. There is no composition curriculum that can begin to compare with the study of scores past and present. Although completed works may appear to be the product of effortless labor, or a miraculous accomplishment that nobody could ever hope to equal, one should not be intimidated by the past. Whatever one's abilities, they should be allowed to mature naturally. One should neither imitate nor emulate a past master (except for study purposes), nor try to shock the unsuspecting world by one's own uniqueness. That uniqueness may well be there. If there is a message worth hearing, the word will get around—there are many ears willing and eager to hear something new if it has substance and is convincingly presented.

It is assumed that the student-reader has already acquired basic musicianship and assimilated the contents of the author's *Music Theory* (two volumes, Oxford University Press, 1961) and *Musical Form* (Houghton Mifflin, 1976).[1] Frequent references are made to the latter, since there are in that text numerous descriptions of compositional structures and possibilities. Here, we are concerned with *prescription* rather than description; with ways and means of starting, continuing, completing, and judging one's own creative efforts.

1. The two texts are indicated hereafter as *KMT* and *KMF*.

Table of Contents

Musical Examples

1. Precompositional Considerations

A painter decides what size canvas to use before applying paint to it. A poet decides in advance the form of a poem, its rhyme scheme (if any), and the metrical structure or nature of the lines. Similarly, a composer determines in advance the probable length of a musical work, the performance medium, the tempo and expressive character, and so forth.

The number of these determinations and the degree of detail with which they are worked out in advance vary according to the work habits of the composer and the specific task at hand. Wagner's original conception of an opera based on the Siegfried legend grew from one to two to three and finally to a cycle of four operas. Beethoven wrote four different overtures (the three so-called *Leonore* and the *Fidelio*) before he finally settled on the latter work to introduce his only opera. On the other hand, Bach's *Goldberg Variations,* an aria and thirty variations for harpsichord, has a plan according to which each third variation is a canon based upon a successively larger interval: thus, no. 3 is a canon at the unison, no. 6 is at the second, no. 9 is at the third, and so on. The first movement of Bartók's *Music for Strings, Percussion and Celesta* opens with a fugal exposition that does not follow the eighteenth-century practice of alternating tonic and dominant entries; rather, the first seven entries (which comprise the exposition) are planned so that numbers 2, 4, and 6 are successively *higher* fifths above the initial entry and numbers 3, 5, and 7 successively *lower* fifths—in the manner of an expanding wedge.

The Wagner and Beethoven examples demonstrate ongoing critical appraisal of a work before it has been "put to bed"; the Bach and Bartók show the result of strikingly imaginative precompositional planning. The two approaches may appear contradictory, but in fact both are needed in the interest of flexibility.

The precompositional considerations and assumptions that should be made are too numerous to list here, and in any case not all of them are relevant to each compositional task. A few representative cases should suffice.

If one is going to compose a fugue, one must first write a subject; that subject is part of the precompositional apparatus. But in the course of writing the fugue, it may become evident—

in order to solve unanticipated problems of harmony, tonality, or connection—that modifications of the fugue subject are necessary. The composer must ask: "Should the original subject be altered, or may variants be permitted?" There is no particular preference for one procedure over the other; one can find examples of both in Bach's *Well-Tempered Clavier,* for instance.[1]

If a rondo is to be composed, presumably the type of rondo (or rondeau)[2] is determined in advance, as well as the overall key scheme and the relationship of subsequent *a* sections to the initial *a* section. While work on the rondo is under way, it may be necessary to alter some of these decisions, and to make new decisions of hitherto unconsidered matters, after playing the work at the piano, hearing the music in one's head (the ideal way to do it), or having the uncompleted work performed.

Style

The style of the work should be determined before a note has been set to paper. The word "style" covers a number of different ideas, and includes such matters as: a) whether the work is tonal, modal, atonal, and so forth; b) whether it is diatonic or chromatic; c) whether it is polyphonic, homophonic, or a combination of the two; d) the harmonic vocabulary used, and the extent to which chords are functional or non-functional;[3] e) the types of non-harmonic tones used or preferred; f) whether the work is "absolute" (concert) music or functional (for dance, theater, cinema, television).

Medium

The medium is the vocal and/or instrumental resources needed for performance. This may be a solo instrument, a chamber ensemble, large orchestra, possibly involving electronic equipment. Occasionally, a work is written simultaneously for two media (as in the case of Brahms's *Variations on a Theme by Joseph Haydn,* composed for two pianos and also for symphony orchestra, both versions published as Op. 56). Ravel is well known for having composed many works both for piano solo and for orchestra, and so skillfully that neither one seems like a transcription of the other. These works of Ravel, such as the *Alborada del gracioso* and the suite *Le Tombeau de Couperin,* like his famous transcription of Moussorgsky's *Pictures at an Exhibition,* reveal the composer as unusually sensitive to the idiomatic use of the performance medium. Bach was quite successful as a transcriber of his own music as well as that of other composers.[4] Beethoven was less successful when he transcribed his *Concerto in D major for Violin and Orchestra* as a piano concerto—a study of the two versions provides a lesson in ill-advised change of medium.

1. See the types of change discussed in *KMF,* page 187.
2. See *KMF,* Chapter 21, for the distinction between these terms.
3. Nonfunctional chords are discussed (and compared with functional harmonies) in *KMT,* Volume 2, chapters 13, 23, 26, 28, and 29.
4. See, for instance, Bach's chorale variation on *Wachet Auf,* originally composed for the cantata of that name, but used again as a work for organ solo (the first of the "Schübler Chorales"), and cited in *KMF,* Example 20.3.

The chosen forces may be balanced, as in a string quartet, or unbalanced, as in a concerto for solo instrument and orchestra. In the former, the four instruments ideally receive equal treatment, though the first violin tends to dominate. One of the most difficult media to handle is the trio for violin, cello, and piano, because the piano (being much stronger than either of the strings) tends to dominate, and violin and cello often team up to attempt a concerted counterbalance.

In the concerto, the virtuoso but acoustically weaker solo provides dramatic opposition to the less virtuoso but acoustically stronger orchestra. It provides a symbol of the "heroic" and active individual in a contest with the relatively faceless and inactive masses. Whether or not this solo-tutti contrast is seen as having psychological or sociological significance, its practice has a long and fascinating history that goes back through the centuries, at least to the responsorial singing in the Christian church and the Hebrew temple, and probably to prehistory, which suggests that this medium has associations that touch many sensitive points in the human psyche.

Motives

Motives can be a great source of unity and continuity. Discontinuation of their use provides separation and contrast. They are not found in all music, however. Examples prior to the Renaissance are rare. Some composers today avoid their use in an attempt to free themselves from a real or an imaginary tyranny, much as composers at the turn of the century felt the need to free themselves from functional harmony and from the controlling reins of tonality.[5]

Motives normally are conceived at the outset of actual composition, and it is useful, at such time, to explore their potentials.[6] Although rhythm is the usual motivic constant, a melodic shape or a succession of intervals *without* a recurring rhythm may be used, as we see in some early Baroque and in some twentieth-century serial music.[7] Motives may be purely abstract, but they also may be used to convey extra-musical associations. Wagner's *Leitmotive* or "leading motives" in many cases (for Siegfried's sword *Nothung,* and for the river Rhine, for instance), seem to try to capture the essence of something objective. More abstract are Wagner's use of the tritone (the *diabolus in musica,* the "devil in music") in connection with the dragon, Fafner; Bach's use of a falling diminished-seventh to suggest Adam's fall in the chorale variation based upon the hymn *Durch Adams Fall;* and the fateful four-note figure used by Beethoven in his *Symphony No. 5 in C minor,* a motive that was taken up again by Brahms in his *Symphony No. 1,* also in C minor.[8]

The structural usefulness of motives may further be observed in the *idée fixe,* in cyclic form, and in thematic transformation. These concepts, usually associated with Berlioz, Franck, and Liszt, respectively, have some elements in common but they may also be distinguished from each other in certain respects. The *idée fixe* is a persistent melodic idea that recurs in several movements of a given work. In Berlioz's *Fantastic Symphony,* it is a symbol of the elusive *femme fatale* who haunts every scene, whether it be the writer's studio, a ball, open fields, or a

5. See *KMF,* Chapter 2, for a discussion of motives in general. See there, also, Example 25.5 for illustration of a melody not based upon motivic development.
6. See *KMF,* examples 2.2 and 2.5, for instance.
7. See *KMF,* Example 2.7.
8. For a description of Beethoven's varied use of this motive, see *KMF,* Example 2.1.

march to the scaffold. Only in the last movement is there much change in the motive; there, in the Witches' Sabbath, it takes on the character of a tormented, twisted caricature.

The term "cyclic form" refers to the end product of inter-movement use of given thematic material, and may be found in many of Franck's mature works, such as the *Symphony in D minor* and the *Sonata in A major for Violin and Piano.* Largely a practice of the late Romantic era, when it was used in connection with the search for new formal procedures, it has precedents in such works of the Classic era as Beethoven's symphonies No. 5 and No. 9. In No. 5, material of the third movement is reintroduced in the course of the fourth; and in No. 9, brief echoes of the first three movements are heard and "rejected" near the opening of the choral finale, as is made clear when the solo bass singer intones the words *"Nicht diese Töne"* ("Not these tones"), and in so doing bridges the gap between dramatic and purely musical necessity.

Thematic transformation, used in extended one-movement as well as in multi-movement works, is often associated with Liszt (see his tone-poem *Les Préludes*). It is a rather subtle device because it involves a change in the outer appearance and character of a theme, while its inner structure is preserved. It is something new that at the same time is not *entirely* new, as a butterfly is but a transformed caterpillar.

Somewhat related to the above, because they are concerned with thematic unity in large-scale works, are the somewhat controversial ideas of the theorist Rudolf Réti. He maintains[9] that in all music by great composers, there are subtle but real relationships between contrasting themes of a given movement and between corresponding themes of different movements of the same work—an idea that seems clearly evident in some instances and rather farfetched in others, but the significance of which should not be ignored, in spite of its apparent lack of universal applicability. Particularly interesting in this connection is the use of a single tone-row in all movements of a multi-movement composition observable in the music of Schoenberg and his followers.

Length

The precise length of a work cannot always be predetermined. But one should be aware that short, moderately long, and large-scale compositions have different characters and ways of using material.

Short works are small but complete musical gestures. They often use compact phrase and period forms and do not proceed far before they begin to move toward their conclusions. The musical ideas are such as not to lend themselves to much development.

Moderately long works contain the seeds of development. Tonal and harmonic structures tend to be multi-layered. Transitions between tonal areas are evident. Modulations become necessary to sustain prolonged interest.

Large works usually make their size apparent at the very outset. Prolonged tonic harmony or extended pedal point may be used, to suggest that we are in no great hurry to move on. Such devices are used by Beethoven at the beginning of his *Symphony No. 9 in D minor* and in Wagner's four-minute Prelude to *Das Rheingold* (sustained E♭-chord to suggest the murky river depths). Postponement of a tonic authentic cadence to the very end creates a long curve

9. See Rudolf Réti, *The Thematic Process in Music,* Macmillan, 1951; and *KMF,* page 324.

(see Debussy's *Prelude to the Afternoon of a Faun* and Brahms's *Piano Concerto No. 2 in B♭ major,* first movement).

In addition to these, there may be inherent qualities of structure (open forms in large works; closed forms, such as the period, in short works) and greater or lesser elaboration of substance that make any particular length seem exactly right. We all know the experience of hearing a work for the first time and noting that an excellent opportunity to end had been missed, or that the music stopped prematurely. Although there is no formula or prescription, in principle a work should end when all the various tensions are resolved, when the various structures in the multi-layered design find their *simultaneous* termination. In *KMF,* Example 8.2(*e*)(2), for instance, the strength of the close of the double period is provided not only by the cadential type—here the strongest of the four cadences—but also (and perhaps this is the reason for the cadential strength) because it is the end of the *three* structural levels: the fourth phrase, the second period, and the group of four phrases. Three arches in the diagram conclude simultaneously, demonstrating the power of unanimous consent. Three orders of tension find their release at a single point. The function here is like that of arches and columns in architecture, and one is reminded anew that architecture has been described as "frozen music."

Mood and character

The mood and character of a work are, of course, not a reflection of a composer's feelings the day the composer sits down to work. The two aspects may emerge from an artist's philosophical outlook and, of course, from traumatic events, such as death and war. However, one has only to read the biographies of well-known composers to realize how little of their everyday lives may be learned from their music alone. Composers, and indeed all artists, live several lives simultaneously. The fortunate ones find that their professional and personal lives are harmonious and complementary. In any case, the chief point to recognize here is that the composer in the very act of creation *makes* the mood. The listener feels the product of creation, not its cause.

A mood may be even and consistent throughout a work or movement. Many Baroque works show the influence of the "doctrine of the affections," which held that a work (or movement) should be unified by reflecting a single emotion. Gradual or abrupt changes of mood generally indicate dramatic or other extra-musical forces at work. When they are extreme, changes of *tempo* and *dynamics* suggest the turbulent emotional states one associates with the Dionysian or "romantic" attitude.

Examples of even and of uneven moods appear in all style periods, the latter more likely to be found from the Baroque era on. In Bach, for example, concerto and dance movements usually display continuous, motoric melodies and rhythms that flow without much interruption or change in dynamics; but there is great dramatic contrast in "So ist mein Jesus nun gefangen" in Part One of *The Passion According to St. Matthew,* where a loud and boisterous chorus (representing an unruly crowd) threatens to drown out the two solo singers.

Webern, in contrast to the perhaps more "classical" Schoenberg, writes tiny movements in which constant changes of tempo, dynamics, and mood create intense concentration and forward propulsion, as if the events of a single day had been crowded into five minutes. Webern's tightness of construction makes such apparently willful and capricious "romantic" expression even more "classical" in orientation than that of the equally "romantic" Berg. This may help explain the more universal appeal of Webern to a generation of post–World War II composers, many of whom searched for a new foundation (for the basis of a new classicism?) as they peered uncertainly into a rather cloudy future.[10]

Tempo

Tempo is a factor that traditionally is relatively uniform throughout a work or movement. As already indicated, tempo, as an element of mood or character, tends to be strict in "classical" works, elastic or variable in works of a more "romantic" persuasion. More than any other musical element, it has in the past tended to provide the basic cast and character to a work; contrasting tempos have been the chief means by which one movement of a composition is distinguished from another.

Once the length has been determined, the composer should select and measure tempo according to the standard metronome indications. If it is decided, for example, that a piece is to be two minutes long, and that the quarter-note equals MM. 60, in a meter of 4/4 there will be thirty measures (2 × 15). Bar lines may then be drawn for the entire work; the composer has made a decision the equivalent of a painter's choice of canvas size.

Of course, this can work perfectly only if tempo and meter are invariable. But even if they do change, pre-barring can provide a useful view of approximate overall length if appropriate adjustments are made.

Contemporary notation sometimes employs spatial indications rather than the traditional means. A parallel development is the use of bar lines to show groups of elements other than metrical units, a practice that recalls the notation of Gregorian chant (where the bar line indicates textual punctuation), the mensural notation of early counterpoint, and the rather erratic barring used in the notation of early organ music.[11]

Except for metronome markings (which are indicated by numerals), tempo and character indications are usually given in the internationally accepted musical language, Italian. However, since Schumann, who introduced German terms, composers have used their native tongue along with the Italian. It is well not to mix them in the same sentence and, whatever one decides to do, to be consistent in the interest of logic and clarity.

Range and tessitura

Range and tessitura are factors of some import, because one's decisions with respect to them affect the character and sometimes the placement of the climax. Range is the distance between the lowest and the highest notes used, tessitura the part of the range most frequently used. Range is, of course, in part determined by the built-in limits of the

10. The terms "Apollonian" (instead of "Classical") and "Dionysian" (instead of "Romantic") may be more appropriate here, since these terms refer properly to artistic tendencies rather than to specific style periods.
11. See the chief guide to standard and contemporary practices, *Music Notation,* second edition, by Gardner Read (Allyn and Bacon, 1964, 1969); and Willi Apel's *The Notation of Polyphonic Music, 900 to 1600* (The Medieval Academy of America, 1942), pages 9–11.

instrument. For most instruments, the lowest note is absolute, but the highest varies according to the ability of the performer. In the piano, of course, the limits are fixed at both ends of the range. There is sometimes a tendency to adhere too much to the mid-register of an instrument, which is an unnecessary deprivation of resources. Unless it is just an exercise in mannerism, it is well to consider, as well, the expressive potentials of the less frequently used "outer fringes" of the range. Stravinsky's use of the unaccompanied bassoon in its high register in the opening measures of *The Rite of Spring* is a striking example of imaginative use of this still relatively unexplored part of that instrument's total range.

A melodic line, or an entire texture, for that matter, may be in a prevailingly low register (tessitura), or a high one, or move from one to another. In the Prelude to Act One of Wagner's opera *Lohengrin,* the design includes motion from soft, very-high-register solo strings at the beginning, to full orchestra *fortissimo* in the middle and low registers, and a close that matches the beginning. The conception underlying the Prelude clearly included the idea of tessitura (an inverted arch) and dynamics (opening and closing wedges)[12] and, of course, preceded the writing of the score.

Another interesting instance of the effective use of tessitura in the design and in the expressivity of a work may be observed in the "Agnus Dei" aria for alto in Bach's *Mass in B minor* (see *KMF,* Example 25.7). First and second violins *unisono* play an obbligato counter-melody to the alto line. They stay for the most part in the same register as the voice and play much the same type of melodic line as is sung, but in the closing measures (45–59), the strings seem no longer capable of controlling their sad feelings, and enlarge their tessitura by plunging down two octaves within four beats (mm. 47–48) in wild and expressive leaps.

Climax

Nothing can be more harmful to a work's overall effect than a poorly placed climax. The point of greatest tension is usually well beyond the middle of a work. If it appears too early, there is an excessively long anticlimax; and if it is too close to the end, the music may appear to stop prematurely.

In most three-part forms, the climax is rather close to the point where part two ends and part three begins. In sonata-form movements, this usually works out nicely, because the retransition that ends the development section characteristically builds up tension by stressing the dominant, tension that is released only by the extended tonic that prevails in the recapitulation that follows. In shorter three-part works, the same principle applies, but there is no need for as much tension as in a larger form. In a rondo form, tension may be created by the use of interpolated development; and in a fugue, climax near the end may be created by the special devices of *stretto* and augmentation.

Even in a single phrase, a deceptive or evaded cadence can provide a certain degree of tension (climax). The tension created by the frustrated (unrealized) cadence is then followed by material of an anticlimactic nature that leads to a realized cadence.

From the above, it may be seen that most music is not based on a single climactic rise and fall, but rather a *series of wave-like motions,* at first piling up ever higher, then gradually ebbing and subsiding. The means of securing these are many. They include dynamics, texture, harmony, tessitura, harmonic rhythm, and orchestration.

12.

Extra-musical factors

Extra-musical factors may influence style and structure, particularly in vocal music, where a text may suggest otherwise unconsidered possibilities. The fourteenth-century Italian composer Landini used canonic imitation in some of his madrigals, the texts of which described hunting scenes or a chase (hence the Italian *caccia* and the English derivation "catch"). An appoggiatura may be associated with grief, a sigh, or a lament. The falling second, in the resolution of this accented dissonance, is rather onomatopoetic in effect.[13] Nineteenth-century *lieder* (art songs) from Schubert on characteristically include vocal and accompanimental substance that is inseparably associated with the text.[14]

Instrumental music displays a parallel development. See, for instance, the imitation of a crowing cock in one of Rameau's harpsichord pieces (readily identified by its title, *La Poule*); Richard Strauss's imitation of bleating sheep and his character portrayals of Don Quixote and Sancho Panza in the tone-poem *Don Quixote,* which is in variation form with elements of a cello concerto as well; Moussorgsky's *Pictures at an Exhibition,* and so on.

Somewhat different from these attempts to turn music into substitutes for painting or literature are works that are influenced by (or descriptive of) ideas or philosophical positions. Observe, for instance, Beethoven's frustrated hopes regarding Napoleon in his *Symphony No. 3 in E-flat* (the "Eroica"); Liszt's *Faust Symphony,* in which each movement is associated in a general way with the characters of Faust, Marguerite, or Mephistopheles; Strauss's tone-poem *Don Juan*, where the episodic and not-too-well-defined amorous adventures of the Don are reconciled with the proprieties of sonata form. Respighi's orchestra in *The Pines of Rome* includes a phonograph, which on cue plays a Victor recording of a nightingale's song. A perhaps related development is the processed sound known as *musique concrète,* which may be used alone or in association with other sounds or noises.[15]

Multi-movement considerations

If there are to be several movements, it is well to predetermine their number, and the tempo and character of each. The overall result may be a suite of stylized dances or one of the "sonata" types (sonata for solo instrument; duo, trio, quartet, or the like; concerto or symphony; and so forth). One may compose a song cycle based on a group of poems or set an extended sacred text of several sections, such as the Mass. Occasionally, one finds an example of mixed species, as in Mahler's *Das Lied von der Erde* ("The Song of the Earth"), which combines aspects of song cycle and symphony; Lalo's *Symphonie espagnole,* really a concerto for violin and orchestra, which displays the developmental procedures one might expect of a symphony; and the aforementioned *Don Quixote* of Richard Strauss, a combination of concerto, tone-poem, and variation form.

The movements may be unrelated (standard procedure) or they may be thematically related by motive usage or the cyclic procedure. They may be connected by a short bridge (see the connections between the three movements of Mendelssohn's *Concerto for Violin and*

13. See "Dido's Lament" in Purcell's *Dido and Aeneas,* and the closing scene (the fool's lament) of Moussorgsky's *Boris Godunov.*

14. See Schubert's *Erlkönig* (*KMF,* Example 25.12), Wolf's *Das Verlassene Mägdlein* (*KMF,* Example 13.9), and Moussorgsky's song cycle *In the Nursery,* for examples.

15. See, for example, Stockhausen's *Gesang der Jünglinge* (recorded by Deutsche Grammophon).

Orchestra, and the thematically anticipatory bridge that leads from the second to the third movement of Beethoven's *Piano Concerto No. 5 in E-flat* (the "Emperor"). Somewhat different from these is a form in which the entire work appears to be one movement of several sections, each of which has different material and tempo; see, for instance, Liszt's *Concerto for Piano and Orchestra in E-flat major* and Weber's *Konzertstück for Piano and Orchestra.* An interesting and rare instance in chamber music is the *String Quartet in C-sharp minor,* Op. 131, by Beethoven, which has seven movements, all played without interruption.[16]

Not to be confused with the above is the occasional use, in separate movements, of an introduction or a coda whose presence is justified largely by the need to relate the movement to its neighbor. Thus, in Dvořák's *New World Symphony,* the second movement, in D♭ major, opens with a modulatory introduction that leads one to this remote key from E minor, the key that closes the first movement;[17] and the "Crucifixus" of Bach's *Mass in B minor,* otherwise in E minor, closes astonishingly in G major, the relative key.[18]

The proper number of movements in a composition, their logical order, possible inter-movement connections, and proper tonal succession are matters that require careful deliberation and planning. There is, once again, no formula for success. The "standard" procedure is no guarantee of merit. Romantic works (see Tchaikovsky's *Symphony No. 6 in B minor*) sometimes end with a slow rather than a fast movement.[19] The grouping slow-fast-slow-fast was common in the Baroque era; fast-slow-fast, in Classic era three-movement works (if there are four movements, the additional one is moderate or fast).

The "center of gravity" should be planned ahead. The "classical" procedure is to put the greatest weight in the first movement (normally in sonata form), the next in weight being the finale. But romantic works, since Beethoven's Ninth Symphony, often put the center of gravity in the last movement. See, for example, the last movements of Bruckner's Ninth and of Mahler's Ninth and his *Das Lied von der Erde.*

One common fault in works of student composers is the writing of first and last movements that are indistinguishable in style and character. It is not enough that they are both fast and enclose a slow movement. The two fast movements should have different weights and functions, contrasting "personalities." Generally, it is best to make the first movement longer (the ears are more willing and patience more lasting), more expansive and developmental, as in sonata form. The finale may be a bit faster, lighter, less "demanding" on one's powers of concentration, more clearly sectional (this eases the demand on the listener's attention span, which may waver if the previous movements have taxed ear and mind), as in rondo form. This is not intended to preclude individuality or variation from accepted practice; rather, it is an attempt to summarize what composers over a long period of time have come to learn about what is musically and psychologically effective.

Intended audience

Which brings us to a consideration of the intended audience. One cannot write for a predetermined audience, as a rule. One may question whether it is proper to write for a

16. See Chapter 26, on "works comprising several movements," in *KMF.*
17. The keys are not as remote as they appear, if one considers D♭ as the enharmonic equivalent of the relative minor of E *major.*
18. This possibly has two explanations: as a musical symbol of Christ's ascent to heaven following the Crucifixion, and as a better lead into the following movement ("Et resurrexit"), which is in D major.
19. See *KMF,* page 327, footnote 12.

particular, given audience. This is a large question, and somewhat beyond our limits here. Our purpose in suggesting the matter is not so much philosophical as it is practical. Music for a small audience (as in chamber music) uses different gestures and rhetoric than music for a large audience (as in opera). Music to be played for a live audience perhaps should be different from music that is heard only via a phonograph, a tape, or on television; here there can be none of the interplay between performer and listener that obtains in the concert hall; the electricity generated by an exciting, virtuoso performance gets lost in the technology if it is not received by the listener and reflected back to the performer, whose sensitive "antennae" pick up that reception and its effect. Performers on radio and television (if there is no studio audience) know this very well—which is the reason for the studio audience.

In addition, one may choose as potential audience one's peers; the sophisticated and experienced concert goers; the young and inexperienced but still open-minded; the mature and conservative; or combinations of these. Naturally, one does not have control over who is going to be present, but there are many types of special audience, and they generally are responsive to the type of music they expect to hear. An avant-garde work is as out of place at a Boston "Pops" concert as *Hair* at the Metropolitan Opera. Given the proper milieu and audience, both types of work may have an opportunity to be well received.

Relation of composition to theory

Finally, does composition follow theory or vice versa? Evidence of both practices appears in the history of music. Greek theories of scales and modes preceded Medieval and Renaissance composition, as twelve-tone theory precedes much twentieth-century music. On the other hand, composers endeavored to use the chromatic scale long before it was practical to do so (i.e., before the tempered scale made it possible to have equal half-steps); and Bach's music, which illustrates so perfectly the principles of root-progression theory, was largely written on the basis of intuition—it is known that he rejected the theories of Rameau on this subject. "Sonata form" as we understand it today is largely a product of the theorists who, in retrospect, formulated its chief characteristics. There is no evidence that the form, as such, was so understood by Haydn and Mozart, despite the fact that they were its chief architects.

In our own age, there are many composer-theorists. Schoenberg, Hindemith, Messiaen, Babbitt, Sessions, Piston, and Xenakis are names that immediately come to mind. Their theories may concern the music of the past, the present, or the future—their own music, largely, or perhaps what music "ought" to be, or could be. It is well to be familiar with the products of these minds, whether or not their theories appear to have immediate applicability—unless, of course, one puts one's trust completely in intuition.

But there is a danger here, too. One might find it useful to adopt (as a kind of professional "security blanket") one or more of the currently fashionable theories, and then spin out compositions that illustrate these theories. Unfortunately, that is what happened to some of the students of Hindemith, a composer who taught at Yale after he left Germany. Students were turning out well-crafted Hindemithiana by the yard, but they did not evolve identities of their own because the theories were too easily learned and assimilated, and because the young composers were not urged to rebel a little and struggle to find their own stylistic paths.

One may classify the style characteristics (in some cases mannerisms or clichés) of a Hindemith, a Webern, a Varèse, or of electronic music; but there is no point in imitating them, except for study purposes. Those studies should always be considered as means of arriving at self-awareness, not as ends in themselves.

One should learn all the theories, study all the scores possible, and experience much music as both performer and listener. Then, one may hope that this "information" will be assimilated and "processed" within. If one has a truly personal thumbprint and good intuitions, something new and valid and interesting will emerge. It is a miraculous process, like life itself. Students, like the caterpillar, may in due time shed their "house" and, like the butterfly, take wing, to add a decorative and perhaps a meaningful contribution to this musically hungry world of ours.

2. Composing a Single Line: Rhythm and Melody

Music is heard linearly, whatever the texture. This is obvious in monophonic and heterophonic music,[1] less obvious but equally true in homophonic and polyphonic music.[2] Since a line characteristically consists of both rhythm and pitch successions, we shall consider each in turn.

The simplest imaginable musical composition is probably one for a single percussion instrument that has no precise pitch, a wood block or snare drum, for example.[3] Our first step, then, is to choose the instrument. Let us decide, arbitrarily, on the snare drum. But before we begin to write a composition for it, there are some questions we should ask and answer, along the lines suggested in Chapter 1: what style do we adopt; what are the sonorous possibilities of this instrument; will there be motives; and so on.

To do this as efficiently and as systematically as possible, we prepare a chart or table of "questions and answers." In your own work, the questions may well be the same as ours, but you may have different answers. Let us now outline the next steps.

1) Keeping in mind the probable dimensions of the measures, rule the bar lines on music manuscript paper.

2) If you did not do so, review the point (m. 20) where the cadenza is to appear; be sure that this measure is large enough to accommodate the needed materials; perhaps allow a whole line, to be on the safe side.

3) Write down, at the beginning, the meter and the MM. indication.

4) On a separate sheet, explore some of the many possibilities for use of the five motives we

1. See *KMT*, Volume 1, Chapter 1, examples I*a* and *b*.
2. See *ibid.*, examples I*c* and *d*.
3. It need not be simple, if extended and combined with another instrument. See, for example, the author's *Sonata for Snare Drum and Piano* (M. M. Cole).

Table 2.1 *Precompositional considerations for a short composition for snare drum solo.*

STYLE	Largely "standard," somewhat exploratory.
METER	5/4
MOTIVES (5 in all)	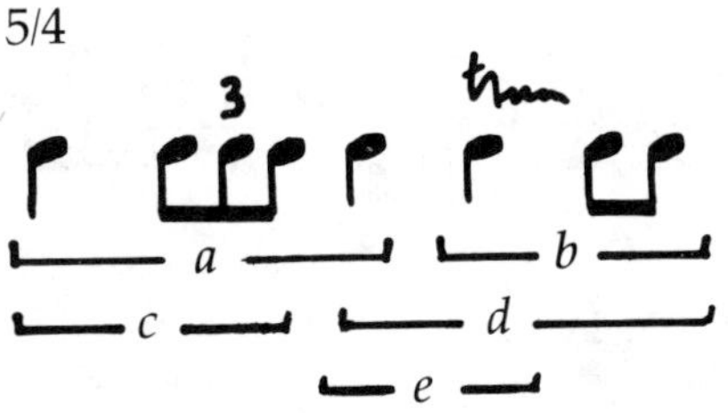 a, b, c, d, e
LENGTH	25 measures. A cadenza will develop near m. 20.
MOOD, CHARACTER	A "modified bolero."
TEMPO	♩ = 120. If there are 25 measures, then (at 25 × 5) there are 125 beats (plus time for the cadenza). The work is thus about one minute in duration.
RANGE	There is no "range," but for contrast, the sticks may occasionally strike the drum on the metal rim, and so forth.
DYNAMICS	From *pp*, crescendo to the cadenza, *ff*. Then diminuendo to *pp*.
CLIMAX	At the cadenza.
EXTRA-MUSICAL IDEAS	None. But the work is somewhat indebted to Ravel's *Bolero*.
AUDIENCE	Concert. Possible encore piece.

have already indicated. These may involve such procedures as repetition; modified repetition (slight rhythm change, change in dynamics, rhythmic displacement, change in tone quality, diminution or augmentation, and so on); or short periods of nonmotivic music.

5) You may wish to note, in pencil, subject to change, where the already-decided-upon dynamics are to be indicated.

These things done, we can now begin to put notes to paper. Keep in mind that this is a short, one-section (one-part) work, of continuous development. Do not make an attempt at binary or ternary structure at this point. Proceed, using the indicated materials, or with material of your own choice. Our own result is shown in Example 2.1.[4]

4. See Exercise 2.1 at the end of the chapter.

Example 2.1 *Composing a short single-line work for rhythm instrument (snare drum solo).*

Without going into a detailed measure-by-measure analysis, let us briefly survey some of the techniques used here. Exact repetition is used only twice, in mm. 1–2 and 11–12. (In the latter case, the crescendo may be regarded as a very minor alteration.) The first repetition presents the motives a second time before we engage in developmental procedures; it also provides some hint of the meter. In m. 3, the *b* and *a* motives appear in that order (the reverse of mm. 1–2). Motivic elision occurs in mm. 3–4, where the fifth beat of m. 3 serves as the last note of motive *a* and at the same time as the first note of *b*.[5] In m. 4, the *a* motive is expanded by a repetition of the triplet fragment, in order to fill out the measure, and for further variation.

In the measures that follow, one may discern one of the motives or another, and occasional use of fragmentation; rests (for contrast and surprise); playing on or near the rim, or a "rim shot," for tone-color contrast; occasional departure from the motives (as in m. 9); a general increase or rise in the dynamic level that is, however, punctuated by some short-term contrasts (mm. 8–10); occasional fall from *f* to *mf* to prevent premature climax; and gradual increase in the number of notes of smaller value, to increase intensity. The use of *a* in diminution (m. 19), in combination with the crescendo, helps us to reach the climax in the cadenza, where we deliberately "lose control" by abandoning the motives. Following the

5. See *KMF*, page 22, footnote 7, Example 3.6*a*, and the index listing, page 336, for explanation and illustration of "elision."

climax in this non-measured bar, there is a reduction in volume, a return to the motives of m. 1, and gradual tapering off to the end, with fragmentation and augmentation in the last measure to suggest final "dissolution."

Readers may wish at this point to examine the work in greater detail, and to perform a similar examination of their own work when it is finished.

The problems that arose during the composition of the work included: 1) how to sustain interest through modified repetition; 2) what kinds of contrast to provide, how much, and where; 3) how to realize the increase of tension building to the climax; 4) what elements to use in the climax, and how to use them; 5) how to bring the work to a close in four measures.

No two people will evaluate the work in exactly the same way. Considering the matters covered in the right-hand column of Table 2.1, I would estimate the work as more conservative than originally conceived. The cadenza occurred in m. 21 rather than 20, which made for a somewhat too-long build-up, and left insufficient time for reduction of tensions. If the work were to be revised, I would place the cadenza a few measures earlier and allow more time for the anticlimax. Ending the work proved to be one of the most difficult parts of the assignment, and not only because of lack of measures, but because somehow the listener must be *prepared* to hear the end. Here we do not have harmony or melody to assist us, so we use what is available. Repetition, rests, and tapering off (*morendo*), which is similar to the use of the vanishing point in visual art, all help. We used only a single "rim shot"; perhaps one or two more, for confirmation, especially in the cadenza, might have been possible.

For our second project, we turn to pitch successions without the element of rhythm. As the denial of rhythmic contrast is a greater deprivation than the denial of pitch contrast, we shall plan a relatively short work, in the table that follows.

Table 2.2 *Precompositional considerations for a short composition using only unmeasured pitches.*

STYLE	Pentatonic scale: C-D-F-G-A.
MEDIUM	Solo voice.
MOTIVES	None.
LENGTH	Short. Impossible to measure details without precise metric indications; bar lines used to indicate elapsed time, 40 seconds.
MOOD, CHARACTER	Abstract vocalise.
TEMPO	Slow.
RANGE	That of a soprano or tenor voice.
DYNAMICS	From *ff* to *pp* to *ff*, the reverse of Example 2.1.
CLIMAX	At the very end.
EXTRA-MUSICAL IDEAS	None.
AUDIENCE	Concert. (Encore piece?)

Let us again prepare our music paper. Draw bar lines to indicate each five- or ten-second time segment. The position of the notes within these "measures" provides some indication of their relative duration.

Example 2.2 *Composing a short vocalise.*

An objective description of the work, beyond the facts listed in Table 2.2, should include the following items:

1) the prevailing falling line during the *ff-pp* measures, rising line during the closing *pp-ff* measures;

2) the use of the comma (') to show breathing points;

3) the irregular appearance of these breathing points, which are necessary from time to time—in contrast to the lack of such need in Example 2.1—unlike the bar lines, which indicate each five-second time-segment;

4) the varying, from measure to measure, of the number of notes in each five-second "bar," and their placement within the bar, to create interest;

5) the relative absence, except in m. 2, of wide leaps, which adds to vocal ease;

6) the climactic "A" at the very end; this may be difficult for some voices, but it is approached gradually and is within the range of a trained soprano voice;

7) the absence of anything one might regard as motivic, except for the "neighboring tone" idea of the last two measures, which is related to the trill;

8) the relatively larger number of notes in the last two measures, which, together with the rise in the line and the crescendo, add to the sense of moving to the climax.

In criticism, one might question the necessity for this type of notation and the lack of vocalization syllables, and perhaps the high note at the end would be easier to perform if it were a step or two lower; the trill is rather difficult for an untrained voice.

Evaluation of your own work, as well as a description of it, is in order when it is completed. (See Exercise 2.2 at the end of this chapter.)

We conclude the chapter with a third project, fully aware that many more projects in this medium could be designed. In it, we shall bring pitch and rhythm successions together.

The most famous examples of extended single-line music are the *Partitas and Sonatas for Unaccompanied Violin* by J. S. Bach. Of somewhat lesser, but still great, interest are his similar but technically less difficult works for solo cello. Not all the movements are written as single-line melodies: many movements contain double-, triple-, and even quadruple-stops, and the use of arpeggiated chords is clearly a way of finding a middle course between the prevailing stepwise motion of melody and the larger intervals found in chords. A melodic line may, by virtue of its principal tones, clearly suggest what the supporting harmonies are understood to be. Arpeggiated chords, where the harmonies are explicit rather than only implied, provide contrast. Careful study of these works, along with contemporary ones (Bartók's for solo violin, Hindemith's for solo viola, and Kodály's for solo cello), might well precede any large-scale endeavors along this line. Meanwhile, we will attempt a short work here, following the customary procedure.

Once the length, meter, and tempo have been decided, a quick calculation indicates that there will be sixty-four measures. We draw bar lines. A not-too-vast, but still considerable, uncharted territory lies ahead. Rather than set off with a fervent hope that our journey will be direct, pleasant, and without complications or disaster, we prepare a sort of itinerary or road map; then, if we get a little off course, we can redirect ourselves before we reach a "point of no return".

Our previous compositions have been arch forms. Let us here, for variety, plan a set of variations, using the first four measures as "theme." Since there are sixty-four (16 × 4)

Table 2.3 *Precompositional considerations for a short work for unaccompanied violin, using single-line melody.*

Style	Bitonal: C and F♯ major.
Medium	Solo violin.
Motives, meter	The leap of a third, rising or falling. Alla breve (2/2).
Length	One minute, 20 seconds.
Mood, character	Lyrical, earnest.
Tempo	Moderately fast. 𝅗𝅥 = 96.
Range	Up to e_3 (E above high C).
Dynamics	No extremes, largely *mf*.
Climax	Shortly past the middle.
Audience	Concert.

measures, there will be sixteen "phrases," of which the first and last will form a kind of frame, similar to Bach's plan in the Chaconne movement of the *Partita in D minor for Unaccompanied Violin*.

Sixteen phrases without subdivision is a bit unmanageable. We might plan groups of four (4 × 4), or an asymmetrical grouping of 5+5+6; or 6+4+6, or 5+6+5, the latter two being symmetrical. We choose the last, thinking of the opening group (5) as a sort of "exposition," the middle group "development," and the final group a quasi-restatement of the opening, but not sufficiently like it to create a ternary design overall. The middle group (6) may be 2+2+2 or 3+3; we shall explore that later.[6]

In the bitonal style we have chosen, we should either integrate the two contrasting scales and keys, or set them off from each other; if the latter, then part of our task lies in exploring the ways of polarizing them. For example, they may be used imitatively, in nearby or in remote registers, in a manner to suggest polyphonic texture; or the two keys may use different materials, albeit that the chief motive of the work is but one; they may be associated with contrasting dynamics, articulation (bowing), and special effects (pizzicato, harmonics, sul ponticello, and so on).

With these additional thoughts in mind, and conditional choices made, let us now begin to compose.

Example 2.3 *Composing a short single-line work for violin solo.*

6. See the similar analyses in *KMF*, page 153, relative to the *Passacaglia in C Minor*, by Bach; and page 155, relative to Bach's *Chaconne in D minor*.

VAR. IV
(f)
B 6 PHRASES
VAR. V
mp subito
VAR. VI
SALTANDO
VAR. VII
PIZZ.
VAR. VIII
P
mf
P
mf
P SEMPRE
VAR. IX
arco
(P) cresc.
f
VAR. X
dim.
C 5 PHRASES
VAR. XI
mf
P
mf
VAR. XII
(III)
mf
mf
mf
P
mf
VAR. XIII
PIZZ.
PP

While the work was in progress, it was noted that, in the two scales, there were two common tones, F (E♯) and B,

C	D	E	(F)	G	A	(B)
F♯	G♯	A♯	(B)	C♯	D♯	(E♯)

the common tones shown here in parentheses. Now we can see that there are two mutually exclusive pentatonic scales, if we *exclude* the common tones, and that the two scales combined, if we *include* the common tones, provide a complete chromatic scale. Also, the two common tones form a tritone, the same interval that separates the two scales.

We decided to suggest the two scales in the opening four-measure "theme" in a manner consistent with our decision to use the leap of a third as a motive. So we arrive at C–E and F♯–A♯ in mm. 1–2. Also, we decide to use all twelve tones in the statement of the "theme." Rhythm contrast is used throughout. An elided cadence is suggested on the first beat of m. 5, where the tonic (C) makes its first reappearance.

Then we plan the variations, as follows:

Var. I: Inversion of the "theme."

Var. II: Retrograde of the two-note groups, thus C-E = E-C, and so on.

Var. III: Largely a transposition of the "theme," but with some rhythmic variations.

Var. IV: Retrograde of the "theme," but rhythmically more animated, except for the fourth (cadential) measure.

The opening five four-measure phrases constituted our first (*a*) group; the six phrases that follow (Var. V-X inclusive) are the second (*b*) group, as planned. They are related to the variations of part *a* as follows:

Var. V derived from "theme."

Var. VI derived from Var. I.

Var. VII derived from Var. II.

Var. VIII derived from Var. III.

Var. IX derived from Var. IV.

Var. X derived from "theme."

In addition, Var. V uses eighth-notes, largely; Var. VI is more intense, with eighth-note triplets; VII and VIII form a group because they use pizzicato and quarter-note triplets (a reduction of tension); IX and X are arco once more, with IX favoring eighth-note triplets and frequent bow changes, and X largely devoted to measured, bowed tremolos in sixteenth-notes.

The final group (*c*) resembles the first group in its mood and character, but the variations are related: XI is derived from IV (it is the retrograde), and there are similar couplings of XII-III, XIII-II, XIV-I, and XV to the "theme." There is thus retrograde motion on two levels: that of the scale degrees (or *pitch classes,* as they are sometimes called) and the order of the related variations in part *a.* There are a number of rhythm changes, designed to provide contrast and a satisfactory close. Despite efforts to avoid an *ABA* or arch form, we do have a sense of that here; but it is more in the understructure than in anything directly perceived.

Again, readers are invited to make additional detailed analysis. More to the point, however, are descriptions of the readers' own compositions.

In evaluating the result of our own work, we see a more-or-less successful attempt to combine bitonality with free chromaticism. It borders on tonality (C is the intended center), but avoids the use of functional tones, such as the leading tone, and harmonic functions, thanks to the ambiguity provided by the frequent tritone relationships. It is rather conservative in the instrumental treatment, calling only for pizzicato and none of the special effects one associates with the avant-garde. The motive of the third, although it appears fairly often, is not used to the point where it becomes insistent: one might be unaware of its prevalence, were it not pointed out. The technical difficulty of performance is moderate; greater demands are made in the realm of musicianship, to bring out the expressivity inherent in the intervals, and the design.[7]

Additional evaluation is invited. And, of course, remember to provide a critique of your own work.

Exercise 2.1 *Using Table 2.1 as a model, prepare a table of precompositional considerations for a short composition for snare drum solo. Write the work so as to be consistent with the original plan, allowing for minor adjustments. In a brief accompanying statement, describe what you have composed and evaluate it to the best of your ability.*

Exercise 2.2 *Using Table 2.2 as a model, and following the suggestions given for Exercise 2.1, compose a work using only unmeasured pitches.*

Exercise 2.3 *Using Table 2.3 as a model, and following the suggestions given for Exercise 2.1, compose a short work for unaccompanied violin.*

---

7. The deliberate effort in Example 2.3 to avoid implied harmonies (through use of the chromatic scale, the tritone, and "assimilated bitonality") may be more clearly observed if we demonstrate, in a short illustration, how mm. 1–2 can be reworked so as to be accommodated to the implied progression, C: I–IV–V–I.

A useful exercise in craftsmanship. The student composer may wish to use this progression as the basis for similar reworking of the variations, which would then become variations on the variations!

3. Composing a One-Part Homophonic Work

It may be assumed that a one-part work is fairly short; that its subdivisions provide little contrast unless strong contrasts are part of the style and design, as in echo effects, dynamically contrasted phrase repetitions,[1] or the expressionist "message," as in our Example 3.2 and some of Webern's miniatures. The composer normally reserves strong cadential punctuation for the end. A unifying motive may be present. In tonal works, modulation is uncommon, but non-functional chords and chromatic harmony may create tonal ambiguity or uncertainty.[2]

For examples, the reader may wish to explore some of the Preludes in Bach's *The Well-Tempered Clavier,* some of Chopin's *Preludes* and *Etudes,* and Bartók's *Mikrokosmos* and two-volume set *For Children*.

In tonal works, the structure is generally no larger than a period or phrase-group.

We attempt two projects in this form, one tonal, the other atonal but not serial.

It is clear from Table 3.1 that our work is to have sixty measures and that the motive is a purely rhythmic one. The pitch content of the motive is variable. The nature of the homophonic treatment is not specified, so we must ask the following questions: 1) Are we to write a melody with a chordal accompaniment? 2) If so, is the melody always above the accompaniment, or may they exchange positions? 3) If they do exchange positions, is there a plan or timetable for these switches? 4) Are the chords to be unbroken or may they be arpeggiated, and, if both, how do we plan for their distribution?

The answers to these and other questions may be written down or simply kept in mind. If one wishes greater freedom, the answers may be deferred until later.

1. See Chopin's *Prelude in C minor,* Op. 28, no. 20, a three-phrase period in which the second consequent phrase is a repetition of the first, but *pp* instead of *p*.

2. See Chopin's *Prelude in A Minor,* Op. 28, no. 2, where the key is uncertain until the final cadence is reached.

Table 3.1 *Precompositional considerations for a one-part homophonic composition in tonal style.*

STYLE	Diatonic.
KEY	C minor.
MEDIUM	Piano.
MOTIVES, METER	 3/4 ♩ | ♩ ♩
LENGTH, TEMPO	About one minute, 𝅗𝅥. = 120 (allegro).
MOOD, CHARACTER	Scherzo. Playful, a bit demonic.
RANGE, DYNAMICS	C below bass staff to E above the treble staff. Variable dynamics.
CLIMAX	At about 40–45 seconds.
AUDIENCE	Concert. Encore piece.

Example 3.1 *Composing a one-part homophonic work in tonal style, for piano solo.*

1) Once the bar lines are drawn, the empty space to be filled presents a challenge. How are we to manage this space? How subdivide it? We could subdivide the sixty-four into symmetrical groups (8 × 8), but this might prove tiresome and predictable. After some experimentation, we arrive at a two-level arch form.

$$\begin{array}{c} (4+6) + (10+12) + (14+8) + (6+4) \\ 10 \quad + \quad 22 \quad + \quad 22 \quad + \quad 10 \end{array}$$

This could be grouped as (10) + (22+22) + (10), with the first ten as introduction or as main statement and the terminal ten as coda. Or as (10+22) + (22+10), which provides a binary mirror form and the necessity for a midpoint cadence. We must make a decision. We choose the first.

2) This decided, we assign a particular texture to each section, identifying them as:

$$\begin{array}{cccc} (4+6) & (10+12) & (14+8) & (6+4) \\ a+b & c+d & e+f & g+h \\ A & B & C & D \end{array}$$

3) Sections *A* and *D* will be harmonically stable, with melody above the harmony. Section *B* will employ chords that are sometimes unbroken, at other times arpeggiated. *C* will be

imitative in style, with the melody sometimes above, sometimes below the frequently arpeggiated chords. A climax should occur in this section, with falling intensity toward the cadence, so that *D* is heard as postcadential, and relatively calm.

4) To ensure a sound harmonic structure, we plan the overall design:

> *A:* tonic pedal point, largely, except for V at the end. In *a,* the chords are to be I, V, I, V, over the pedal point. In *b,* we use IV, V-of-V, then an extended V.
>
> *B:* bass line to move chromatically *upward* from the tonic in part *c, downward* chromatically from C to G in part *d,* dwelling on the dominant at the end of *B* to create a half-cadence.
>
> *C:* the prevailing harmonic motion is such that the roots progress alternately *up* a fourth and *down* a third in part *e,* to prepare for the cadence in part *f.*
>
> *D:* an authentic cadence is to elide with the beginning of part *g.* Continuing motion will serve as postcadential extension. Part *h* provides harmonic stability, and may involve no chords other than the tonic.[3]

5) With this plan, we have in effect a blueprint for the tonal structure. We are prepared to put notes to paper. As we proceed, we check to be sure our vision was both capable of realization and esthetically satisfying. If there were miscalculations, we make mid-course adjustments and then continue.

6) The *A* and *B* sections (*abcd*).

First, we write the pedal point and indicate the motive, in *a.* Intervals in the left-hand part expand texture in *b;* bass moves to c:V; motive is developed in the right hand.

In *c,* we write the chromatic bass line first; then we plan the harmonies (series of secondary dominants), the rising mel-

3. For explanation and illustrations of postcadential extension, see *KMF,* pages 76–79, and Example 19.10 (mm. 29–31).

ody line in right hand; finally, the chord tones above the bass, editing (slurs, dynamics). In mm. 19–20 the texture changes to prepare for the broken-chord eighth-notes in *c*.

From m. 21, broken chords in the right hand, motive in the left hand, softer.

Again, the bass is written first; in mm. 25–27 we approach the dominant, G; we repeat it with its upper neighbor, in a series of augmented-sixth chords that resolve to V. This is an extended half-cadence.

7) The *C* and *D* sections (*efgh*).

The motion continues, in *e*, in one voice or another. First, we write the bass line, following the "recipe"; to avoid excessive root-position chords, many of these bass tones are used as chord-thirds in first-inversion triads. Next, the running eighths, to provide harmony; finally, the motive, used imitatively. For relief, scale-lines in mm. 37–40. Climax reached, m. 44.

The cadence in m. 47 is *weakened by the double suspension,*[4] an idea that seemed worth continuing in section *f*. The bass line, now all dotted halves, descends chromatically from C to G.

4. See *KMT*, Volume 1, Chapter 28, Example I*e*, for explanation and description of this term; and *KMF*, Table 4.2, "Factors affecting the weight of a cadence."

Section *D* functions as coda. In *g* we transfer the double ties over the bar line to the left hand, after writing the bass line (twofold descent, diatonic, from C to G). Hemiola[5] is used in r.h. line; middle line engages in imitation while filling out the harmonic and rhythmic needs for balance. Section *h* is over tonic pedal like *a*, a final extension, I-IV-I, with "fade-out" in closing statement of motive, unharmonized.

Evaluating the finished work, one can see that, though brief, it contains many notes and the texture is at times rather "busy," particularly at the indicated tempo. With a little tailoring, it would suit a string quartet very nicely, perhaps better than piano, largely because of the imitations, which are less clear and digitally more cumbersome on the piano. A slower tempo might be advisable.

The character derives somewhat from Beethoven, and the choice of chords is reminiscent of some of the variations in that composer's *Diabelli Variations,*[6] Op. 120, and the *32 Variations in C minor,* Op. (posth.) 191. Once again there is a suggestion of arch form, but the planned binary structure, a somewhat expanded two-phrase period, is clear enough. We took care to

5. Hemiola is a rhythmic device in which two measures of 3/4 meter become, in effect, a single measure of 3/2 (or three measures of 2/4), for example:

3/4

or

(= 2/4).

6. See *KMT,* Volume 2, Example F.

vary the motive's intervallic contour, to avoid monotony: sometimes it ascends, sometimes descends. Occasionally, all the notes are chord tones; sometimes the note on the downbeat is a suspension. In part *d,* use of the motive every other measure instead of every measure provides contrast. The grouping of two beats in the right hand in mm. 26–28 against the threes in the left hand is an implied metrical contradiction that helps create tension; balance is restored by the rhythmic sequences that follow.

Section *e,* as indicated, is texturally too complex, perhaps a bit inconsistent with the character of the work, and it strays from our plan to write a homophonic piece. It was not necessary to follow our original plan with absolute rigidity; but enthusiasm of the moment carried us away. A useful project would be the reconstruction of this section, adhering more closely to the texture of the surrounding sections.

In any case, a similar project should be worked out by the reader. The several steps should be checked in consultation with the teacher as the composition unfolds.

The second project in this chapter is the writing of an atonal (but not serial) work, again homophonic in texture. To facilitate comparison, we shall write this also for piano, but change many of the other factors.

Table 3.2 *Precompositional considerations for a one-part homophonic composition in atonal style.*

STYLE	Atonal, expressionistic.
MEDIUM	Piano.
METER, MOTIVES	In C(4/4). Major sevenths, minor ninths, and their inversions.
LENGTH	30 seconds.
TEMPO	Slow, ♩ = 48.
MOOD, CHARACTER	Dark, somber; a bit violent.
RANGE, DYNAMICS	Tessitura in low or high register, avoiding the middle. Contrasting *pp* and *ff,* no *mf.*
CLIMAX	At the beginning. Gradual decay.
EXTRA-MUSICAL IDEAS	Might be useful as modern dance solo or *pas de deux.*
AUDIENCE	Concert or theater.

This work, although short, can be very effective if the strong contrasts are properly worked out. The duration may prove too short; if necessary, we shall extend it. To ensure atonality, it would be well, as we proceed, to use the chromatic scale degrees with approximately equal frequency. This can be checked as we move along, by using a "box score" arrangement. Motives will appear regularly but not insistently, and we shall endeavor to avoid the temptation to be polyphonic!

Example 3.2 *Composing a short one-part homophonic work in atonal style, for piano solo.*

We plan each measure so as to use all twelve tones, in no particular order, but always with emphasis upon the motivic interval. We employ rhythmic freedom and a quasi-improvisational style, avoiding rhythmic repetition. We block off dynamics to form four groups, as we proceed—*ff, pp, ff, pp.* We try to avoid the middle register. Occasional use of sustained or repeated notes, for contrast. Rests for separations. When the work was nearly complete, the need for greater separations seemed evident, so the fermatas were added in mm. 2 and 5. The first of these helped to separate the *ff* from the *pp* phrase, the second to separate the second *pp* phrase (m. 4) from the *ff* phrase that follows. Observe that there is no need for a fermata on the first beat of m. 4—the texture and tessitura change is sufficient; and at the change of dynamics in m. 6, there is a deliberate overlap—the bass entry is almost inaudible. (This should be carefully observed in performance.) In the final measures, the intervals of the second and seventh form clusters (*à la* Ives and Bartók). The final fermata is "rhetorical" in effect: the performer should keep hands close to keyboard.

What are the measuring sticks for the evaluation of such a piece? We may consider the degree of success with which the intentions have been realized. But evaluation is inevitably somewhat subjective—the critique is to a degree a reflection of the taste of the observer.

Looking at the piece objectively, we detect a touch of polyphony in mm. 2–3, but by and large there are either chords or clusters, or a melodic line accompanied by such agglomerations. The motives are more foundations of chords than elements essential to the progress of the melodic lines. After all, invariable use of these intervals would have become obsessive and tiresome in short order.

This suggests an interesting comparison with the previous example. There, the single motive is more complex, and rhythmic rather than intervallic. By definition, it is more flexible. This built-in flexibility is an asset the value of which can hardly be overestimated. It would be well to remember the significance of built-in flexibility when the time arrives for us to compose still larger and more complex works.

We have succeeded in escaping from arch form. Indeed, the form is rather through-composed. The four dynamic groups (*ff, pp, ff, pp*) are in decidedly asymmetrical balance (1½+2½+1+1), and we therefore cannot realistically see the four as 2+2, or the six measures as 4+2.

The unusual climax at the beginning is never seriously challenged in the following measures. But the second *ff* does provide a useful nadir, in balance, prior to the evaporation in the ensuing morendo.

This density and concentration help to satisfy us despite the piece's brevity. Expansion would require additional contrast of texture and style to sustain interest.

It goes without saying that these two projects only suggest the *procedure* to be followed in writing a short homophonic work in one part. We do not mean to imply that compositions of this type are what the student composer *must* end up with.

The student should devise various precompositional plans in detail before committing notes to paper. Student and teacher, in close collaboration, should weigh the implications of these plans. Then, as the work is revised, scrubbed, and polished, and unfolds, carefully edited with slurs, dynamics, and so forth, the student must determine the point at which nothing remains to be done—except to secure a performance. After which, the composer may deem alterations necessary. The reasons for these changes should be filed away in one's memory, where they may be recalled in future planning.

Additional design possibilities for one-part works may be found in *KMF*, chapters 7–9. Not all the examples cited there represent complete pieces or movements. However, Example 7.16 shows the relatively complete one-part Trio portion of a compound ternary form,[7] as does Example 7.22, which, however, is more a small ternary form. (Comparison of these two would be a useful study at this point.) The abstract forms shown in examples 8.1 and 8.2 may be effectively used in a slow tempo. The Appendix of *KMT*, Volume 2, examples A and J, illustrate quite different aspects of one-part form, and could also serve as models for original compositions.

Exercise 3.1 *Using Table 3.1 as a model, and the two-column procedure of Example 3.1 as a work method, compose a one-part homophonic work for piano in tonal style. As in previous exercises, describe and evaluate your music once it is completed.*

Exercise 3.2 *Using Table 3.2 as a model, and the two-column procedure of Example 3.2 as a work method, compose a one-part homophonic work in atonal style. Follow the procedures suggested in Exercise 3.1, to prepare, and then to describe and evaluate your work.*

7. See Chapter 8, and *KMF*, Chapter 14, for explanation and illustration of this form.

4. Composing a One-Part Polyphonic Work

One-part form, we have already indicated, is relatively uncommon in music. In polyphonic music, examples may be found in rounds,[1] such as "Row, row, row your boat," and in chorale-variations based upon short hymns, such as Bach's "Meine Seele erhebt den Herren" in *Six Schübler Chorales.*[2] See also the canons in Bach's *Musical Offering,* some of the short pieces by Bartók cited on page 23, some of the miniature movements by Webern,[3] and some of the Interlude movements in Hindemith's *Ludus Tonalis.*[4]

The procedures for writing a chorale variation based upon a two-phrase hymn tune are displayed in some detail in *KMF*, Example 20.11, where there is a discussion of the treatment of the aforementioned "Meine Seele erhebt den Herren," one of Bach's *Six Schübler Chorales.* The ten-measure tune is set to a fugal accompaniment that includes a prelude, interlude, and postlude. Although there are two phrases, the work is one-part because the first phrase ends on III, the second on I—the design is thus an expansion of period form.[5]

A rather long one-part polyphonic form in canonic style may be found in *KMF,* Chapter 17, Exercise 1. There are five phrases in each of the canonically related upper voices; the canon is in inversion; the phrases are separated by rests; there is a quasi-ostinato figure in the bass; and the following modulatory scheme is used: d-F-e-F-d. This is a group of phrases closely related in substance and style, but not related to period form. Modulations provide contrast. Continuity of material and momentum and the overlapping phrases that result from canonic texture help to ensure one-part form. By way of contrast, the somewhat similar third

1. See *KMF,* page 159.
2. See *KMF,* Example 20.11.
3. Webern's *Five Pieces for Orchestra,* Op. 10, fourth movement (1913), is only six measures long!
4. Some of the Bartók, Webern, and Hindemith movements are homophonic, some polyphonic, some in mixed style.
5. See *KMF,* Chapter 8, "Extension of the Period."

movement of Bach's *Sonata No. 2 in A major for Clavier and Violin* has a form that may be regarded as either two-part with coda, or as incipient three-part.[7]

Our projects in this chapter are concerned with ways and means. First of all, we should make our commitments in a precompositional chart, secondly, put bar lines on our manuscript paper. For contrast, let us plan one project in imitative style, the other non-imitative.

Table 4.1 *Precompositional considerations for a one-part polyphonic work in imitative style.*

STYLE	Tonal, major mode, diatonic, figured-bass (rather than root-progression) oriented.
MEDIUM	Woodwind trio.
MOTIVES	Motive(s) derived from opening.
LENGTH	Three phrases; about 45 seconds.
MOOD, CHARACTER	Calm, serene.
TEMPO, METER	Moderato, 5/4 meter. ♩ = 80.
RANGE, DYNAMICS	Middle and low registers of each instrument. Largely *mf*.
CLIMAX	Moderate climax, around the middle of the third phrase.

A few more matters before we rush into musical notation. At MM. ♩ = 80, forty-five seconds of music involves sixty beats (three-quarters of eighty). In 5/4 meter, that adds up to twelve measures. Now we can draw the bar lines. Number measures on the three-system score; each instrument has its own line. We decide the instrumentation: flute, oboe, and bassoon. They are not exactly equal, since the oboe is naturally a more penetrating instrument.[8] The key: C major. Will the three phrases be equal or unequal in length? To avoid exact symmetry we decide on 5+3+4 (=12). Will the instruments all play together in m. 1, or will they enter in turn? We decide on the latter, with the order: flute, bassoon, oboe, taking into account that the oboe will easily be able to "cut" into the texture to make its presence known. Now, we are ready.

6. See *KMF*, examples 16.8 and 17.2.
7. For explanation and illustration of these forms, see *KMF*, chapters 11 and 13.
8. The oboe gets softer and thinner the higher it goes, whereas the flute gets louder and more penetrating. The observation above refers to the middle register of each.

Example 4.1 *Composing a one-part polyphonic work for woodwind trio, in imitative style.*

First, the flute enters, with the motive, on C, in m. 1. The bassoon enters in m. 2, on G. We then continue the flute line to m. 2, beat 2, where it comes to rest. We mark this entry and all motive entries with a bracket. The counterpoint in the flute continues in m. 2; we try to secure linear contrast to the bassoon line. Should the oboe start on C or G, and on which beat? We decide, and write out the motive. We then continue the bass line, to have a good foundation; then add the flute part. An additional entry in the bassoon is written in, altered at the end so as to finish in m. 5, as planned. Then the flute line, to the cadence, end of m. 5. Last, the oboe.[9]

To help clarify the phrase structure, we thin out the texture in m. 6. For contrast, we

9. Although the music is conceived in figured-bass style, the figures are omitted. In m. 5, for instance, were they added, they would read as follows:

98 6 65 45 3.
43 3- 23

There is a double suspension on beat 1 and an appoggiatura on beats 3 and 4. The "3" on beat 5 normally is omitted because understood.

use the motive in inversion and begin on a note other than C or G. Different order of entries. Since this phrase is short, stretto seems like a good procedure to use. Oboe is first, since it was the last in phrase 1. The F♯ provides a secondary dominant, not a modulation. Flute entry follows, at the octave, and is varied so it fits. The F♮ is put in at once, to restore unambiguous C major. Bassoon entry is added, with continuation, in contrary motion, to the cadential G, which is C:V. The flute, then oboe, continue through m. 8.

In the third phrase, we let the bassoon begin, since it has not previously been first. All entries now begin on C, to balance phrase 1, and to emphasize the tonic key. To be sure our cadence is effective, we work out the final oboe entry, *backwards* from m. 12. Then continue the bass line to the very end. We complete the oboe line, and help reach the climax in m. 10. By sheer luck, the flute can play the motive in m. 10, and provide at the same time the needed chord tones. We continue to the end, then re-check to be sure all is completed, editing included.

A description of the work would note that the melodic lines are largely stepwise; leaps appear chiefly at breathing points, except for the chord outline in the bassoon (m. 3). As a result, chords are largely a product of the lines, and, except at cadential points, are not influential in determining the melody notes. Chords are largely triadic. There are a few passing tones, and several appoggiaturas; in m. 5 there is a double suspension on the first beat. There are no changes in the dynamics: the register-changes in the instruments provide the contrast. The tempo at the very end might be broadened by a slight ritenuto. There is some sense of ternary design because of the departure from tonic-dominant entries and the use of inversion in the second phrase, but the work is essentially one-part.

In criticism, the piece may be regarded as a little bland, without much color, despite the use of three different instruments. There is no attempt to capitalize on those idiosyncracies that distinguish one instrument from another. Its rhythmic freedom, which ensues naturally from the quintuple meter (which is sometimes 3+2, sometimes 2+3) is less apparent than the somewhat academic use of the motive, which seems, in retrospect, to make the piece rather an exercise. It does not seem to have very much to "say" to us.

For our second project we will try, as always, for something quite contrasting. We start with a table.

Table 4.2 *Precompositional considerations for a one-part polyphonic work in non-imitative style.*

STYLE	Chromatic, improvisatory, atonal.
MEDIUM	String trio.
MOTIVES	None.
LENGTH	One phrase, about 45 seconds.
MOOD, CHARACTER	Mysterious, fleeting.
TEMPO, METER	Very fast. No meter. Bar lines indicate each 2 seconds of elapsed time.
RANGE, DYNAMICS	Wide range for each instrument, *pianissimo* throughout.
CLIMAX	Practically none at all.
SPECIAL EFFECTS	Harmonics, snap pizzicato (*à la* Bartók), con sordino, sul ponticello, col legno.
INTENDED AUDIENCE	Concert, or as background music for film or dance.

First steps involve preparation of our manuscript paper, showing the three systems, instruments, and bar lines to show the two-second segments. Since there will be no beat to follow, some means must be found by which the performers can stay reasonably together. Either they will all play from the full score, there will be cues in their individual parts, or there will have to be a conductor to mark the passage of each time segment. This should be decided in advance, because if full score is to be used in performance, the size of the page and of the notes must be taken into account.

For forty-five seconds of music we need twenty-two or twenty-three bars of two seconds duration. We allow enough space for a large number of notes, since the piece is to be in a fast tempo. The style of notation must now be decided. We borrow from conventional notation, with the understanding that note values are not to be construed as absolute; the space between the note-heads serves as some indication of their relative duration; placement within the bar indicates relationship to the other instrumental lines. Exact coordination can be expected only on "downbeats." We jot down ideas for the first four seconds (two bars).

Example 4.2 *Composing a one-part polyphonic work for string trio, in non-imitative style.*

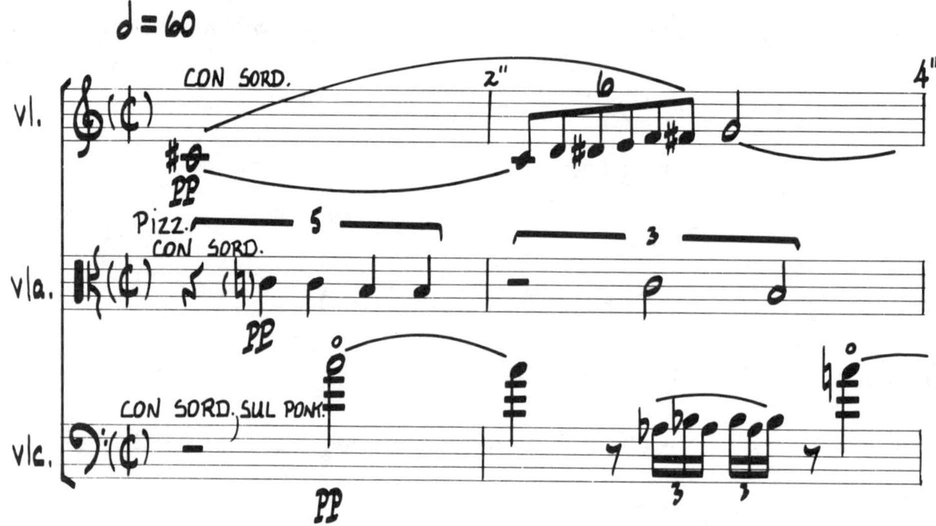

Rather than proceed totally without knowing which notes to use (or not use), we again decide to use all twelve chromatic notes within a given space, in this instance two bars. We start with the violin, outline a tritone (which helps to create tonal ambiguity), and fill in with chromatic half-steps. The viola plays pizzicato, and with contrasting rhythm, only the two notes C and B. The remaining notes are in the cello, playing sul ponticello; the high A is a natural harmonic. We thus get three different tone colors as well as contrasting lines and rhythms. We started without meter indication, but this seemed at once like an unnecessary deprivation: the same results are achieved by using conventional notation, so we add a time signature (₵) and then continue.

We tie over the notes in the violin and cello lines. The violin continues to rise chromatically, in mm. 3–4, but in minor ninths rather than seconds, augmenting the triplet idea, which we borrow from the viola line, m. 2. Continuing our use of all twelve tones each two measures, the viola line descends in a varied sequence of its first measure; the cello repeats the neighboring-tone idea before it outlines consecutive sevenths (which are nothing but octave displacements of consecutive whole steps) with varied retrograde repetition following in the next measure.

The idea of rhythmic counterpoint continues in m. 5. The violin is very active at first, then sustains its last note (D) to provide a sort of anchor. The triple-stop pizzicato provides contrast without adding any new scale degrees. The viola is quite stable, almost a pedal point on E. The cello, in a large arch, plays only E♭ and F; the distinction between the rhythms of mm. 5 and 6 is very subtle, and to make this clear we add the accents.

Feeling the need for more tension, we increase the number of small notes, continuing the strong rhythmic contrast. The tonal prolongations in the violin and viola in m. 8 help provide some stability and parallel the procedure used in m. 6. The use of three-against-five in the upper parts provides both consistency and contrast. Continued use of pizzicato ensures lightness as well as color.

Consistent use of whole steps, rather than half, unifies these two measures; one of the results is a whole-tone scale in the violin.

Mm. 9–10 continue the avoidance of simultaneity to a large extent, preferring triplets and quintuplets. We use wide leaps and dissonant intervals that do not suggest chord formations. Once again, now in the viola, a subtle rhythmic distinction: (vs. ).

We are now almost at the midpoint. Using the arch or mirror principle, we shall repeat the music in retrograde, adding on two measures at the end in such a manner as to provide a satisfactory close.

11
22"
24"
26"
Pizz.
arco
sfz
PP
14
28"
32"
arco
(PP)
mf
sfz
17
8VA
32"
34"
36"
Pizz.
sec.
(PIZZ.)
SUL PONT.
arco

Here and there, it will be observed, the precise retrograde has been changed, usually to facilitate performance.

Our use of triplets and quintuplets has a curious result in the retrograde motion, since notes of equal value are the same: and are unaltered, as in a palindrome, and thus are a reflection in miniature of the structure of the work as a whole. Olivier Messiaen, in *The Technique of My Musical Language*, refers to these as "nonretrogradable rhythms" because no change occurs in the retrograde.[10]

To secure a sense of finality, we use augmentation of note values and extension by means of repetition in the last two measures. For additional sense of repose, fermatas are used in the last measure.

Once again, it may be thought that we have a binary (two-part) form. In fact, the two halves make one whole, perhaps not in the same manner as the two phrases of a period, but in that there is a single, large gesture, comprising a rise and a fall, like an upbeat and a downbeat.[11]

The observant reader may have noted that we did not decide on the subdivisions of this work prior to the start of composition, unlike our procedure in previous exercises. We decided to retrograde the first ten measures only upon arrival at m. 10. We leave to the reader the evaluation of this procedure; at any rate, one product of that delayed decision is the absence of marked points of division such as we find in Example 4.1.

There may be some who regard this "solution" to the "problem" of form to be an easy one. But retrograde does not always "work"; it must be tested and, as in the present instance, altered if musically necessary. Besides, precedents for such structural categorical imperatives may be found in the *da capo* aria[12] and the formal repetitions characteristic of small and large

10. Olivier Messiaen, *The Technique of My Musical Language,* translated from the French by John Satterfield, Alphonse Leduc (Paris), 1956.
11. For a comprehensive study of the relationship of rhythm to form see Grosvenor W. Cooper and Leonard B. Meyer, *The Rhythmic Structure of Music,* University of Chicago Press, 1960.
12. See *KMF,* pages 312-313 and Example 25.9.

binary forms.[13] Schubert wrote many of his piano-sonata first movements only up to the beginning of the recapitulation, whose key scheme IV-I, seemed to him an obvious transposition of the exposition section's I-V and therefore in no need of notation—clearly Schubert had not yet arrived at the view that recapitulations *must* begin in the tonic!

The whole question of repetition in music, whether exact or varied, is a large one, particularly at the present development of the art. Some composers feel that repetition, particularly if it is *expected,* is an infringement upon their artistic freedom. The psychological value and significance of repetition has never been fully explored. Questions to be considered include the reasons for repetition, the degrees of variation possible within the limits of comprehension, and the possible value of repetition that is varied to the degree that it is no longer recognizable as such. Whether our repetition in retrograde is a success or not, we leave to the reader to decide.

Exercise 4.1 *Using Table 4.1 and Example 4.1 as guide or model, compose a one-part polyphonic work. Be sure to describe and evaluate the finished product.*

Exercise 4.2 *Using Table 4.2 and Example 4.2 as guide or model, compose another one-part polyphonic work. The style should be different from that used in Exercise 4.1. Describe and evaluate your work.*

13. See *KMF,* Example 14.1.

5. Composing a One-Part Work in Mixed (Homophonic-Polyphonic) Styles

Some music is not consistently homophonic or polyphonic, but either mixes the two styles at once or uses them in different sections as a means of securing contrast. The finale of Mozart's *String Quartet in G major,* K. 387, for example, utilizes fugal procedure for both first and second themes in the exposition section of a sonata form, and then relaxes into a more familiar homophonic style in the closing theme.

Larger forms, such as sonata and rondo, commonly employ polyphonic procedures in development sections or in interpolations, in contrast to the main tissues which for the most part are homophonic. In the last movement of Walter Piston's *Sonata for Violin and Piano,* a largely homophonic rondo form, an interpolated fugato creates an interesting departure from the listener's expectations.[1] The somewhat "homogenized" use of both types of texture may be observed in *KMT,* Volume 1, Example I*e*. In Mozart's *Piano Sonata in D major,* K. 284, third movement, a variation form, the theme and most of the variations are homophonic, but some are in mixed style (variations 6 and 8), and variation 9 is clearly polyphonic (in two voices) with suggestions of canonic imitation.[2]

We shall now attempt to write an example, in which—within a one-part framework—we employ a variety of textures. Our plan is to compose a three-phrase period[3] in which phrase 1 is homophonic, phrase 2 is polyphonic, phrase 3 a mixture. There will be one antecedent phrase and a double-consequent, the first phrase ending on a half-cadence, the others ending with authentic cadences. The period will be tonal and harmonically structured, which is to say the chief chords will be predetermined. The medium: organ (may also be played piano four-hands).

1. For details, see *KMF,* Example 22.2.
2. See the excerpts cited in *KMF,* Example 15.10.
3. This form is discussed in *KMF,* pages 62–64 and illustrated in examples 7.13, 7.14, and 7.15.

Example 5.1 *Composing a solo for organ: the first phrase.*

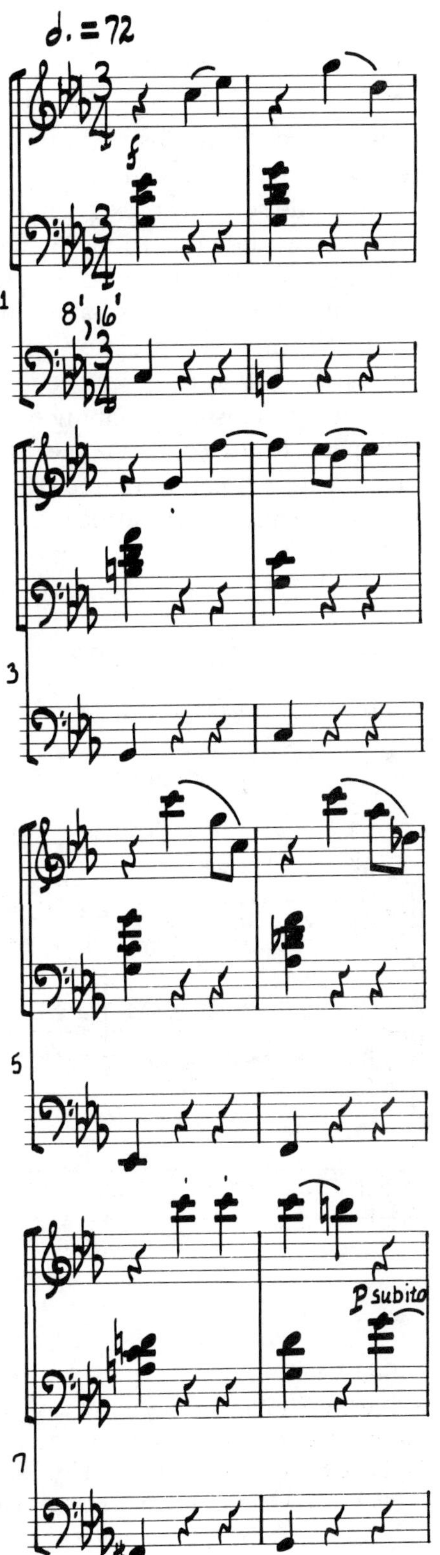

We think about first the length: we decide to have three eight-measure phrases. the tempo: 𝅗𝅥. = 72 in 3/4 meter. The key: C minor.

For phrase 1 we decide on the harmonic structure and rhythm as follows:

I	V6	V7	I (+)	I6	IV7	V7-of-V	V
𝅗𝅥.	𝅗𝅥.	𝅗𝅥.	𝅗𝅥.	𝅗𝅥.	𝅗𝅥.	𝅗𝅥.	𝅗𝅥.

Dynamics will be *forte* throughout. The motive is to be | 𝄽 ♩ ♩ | with supporting chords on the downbeat. These decisions made, the music almost writes itself.

We take care to vary the motive, so it sustains interest. In mm. 4–6, the use of eighths instead of quarters provides such variation. In m. 3, the notes are detached instead of slurred, and the suspension provides a two-measure group as relief from excessive repetition of one-measure units. We take care to watch the fundamental line[4] of the melody (C-G-F-E♭+C-B); in the second half, there are secondary lines in the middle register (C-D♭-D♮) and in the bass (E♭-F-F♯-G). We are careful with voice leading and doubling; the suspension and appoggiatura resolution tones are carefully *not* doubled. The tie over the bar line (mm. 8–9) ensures continued motion and prepares for the change in texture.

4. 

Our plans for the first consequent phrase include: *piano* dynamics, two-voice texture without the pedals, some running eighths for contrast, continued use of the motive (needed for unity of the period form); and a harmonic scheme: { VI | IV | VII | III (+) V6-of-IV | IV | V | I } in which there are clearly four two-measure groups with VI going to IV, VII to III, V-of-IV resolving to IV, and V to I.

Since the second consequent will (or *should*) be a varied repetition of the first consequent,[5] we plan it ahead also, along with the first consequent. It will have the same harmonic structure, but it will be *forte*, like the antecedent. The style will resemble both antecedent and consequent 1, and thus have a mixture of homophonic and polyphonic textures. This is a kind of formal compression, in which one section presents in itself what had previously appeared in two or more sections.[6] It is clear that the music ends abruptly. To provide a satisfactory close, we change our original plan, and add a four-measure postcadential extension to the second consequent phrase, which shall repeat the previous four measures but, through means still undetermined, in a more forceful manner (increase in dynamics, or sudden *piano*, might suffice; or perhaps octave transposition, as an echo effect).

To facilitate comparison, we put the two consequent phrases in adjoining columns.

Example 5.2 *Composing a solo for organ: the second and third phrases.*

(First consequent) (Second consequent)

9 17 (8', 16')

f subito

5. See *KMF*, page 62.
6. See the Stravinsky *Sonata for Two Pianos*, first movement, mm. 73–86, in which the second theme is a *one*-phrase compression in the recapitulation if it is compared with the *two*-phrase statement in mm. 17–52 of the exposition (see *KMF*, Example 23.5). In the final movement of Brahms's *Symphony No. 1 in C minor*, development and recapitulation are compressed into a single section.

(First consequent)
(Second consequent)
11
19
13
21
15
23

(Postcadential extension)

In the first half of the first consequent, we have a grouping of 2+2, as planned, in which the running eighths provide counterpoint to the motive, with exchange of pattern every measure, and alternations of ascending and descending eighths. In the second half, the running eighths continue, but alternate every two measures; meanwhile, the motive is used in a hemiola rhythm. The continuing motion weakens the cadence.

In the second consequent, the first half recalls the texture and dynamics of the antecedent while adhering, as we indicated, to the harmonies of the first consequent. The chords are all in first inversion. The second half features a return of the running eighths, and the accompaniment is animated to suggest a more linear (polyphonic) texture, with the eighths remaining in the soprano line throughout. The cadence in m. 24 is weak, as anticipated; and to ensure its weakness, we continue the motion.

The postcadential extension, when we arrived at that point, seemed to require more harmonic tension than would have been provided by the chords of mm. 21–24. We therefore used a Neapolitan sixth in m. 25, and the very helpful cadential I^6_4-chord in m. 26, prior to the final V-I. Reduction in the dynamics not only provided contrast, but also served as a reminder of the first consequent phrase. Observe that in these last measures, we use both the main motive and the running eighths, which have become a secondary motive through extensive use.

The student composer should plan a similar work, not necessarily in a similar style. The means of securing both unity and variety should be given careful consideration. The work as a whole should be created in abstract, as a vision, with structural lines or procedures determined in advance. As in the work we have just observed, alterations may be made, provided there is good reason.

A work of this brevity should be written in a single day, even in a single sitting, if possible. If the preliminary work has been properly accomplished, the writing should proceed rapidly. Nothing stops the creative impulse more than *not* knowing what to do next; once motion is begun, the pen should be allowed to move without debilitating stoppages. This is not a matter of sentiment, but a practical recommendation. A tennis player or a golfer knows how important is the follow-through motion. A similar principle applies here.

The critical and evaluative faculties should not be allowed to interrupt this flow. They may assist it, or redirect it. But the best time to exercise those skills is when the work has reached the end, in first draft. Repeated performance or listening with one's inner ear may suggest improvements here and there. If many substantial alterations are made, so that the composition becomes a patchwork, it may be well to scrap the first effort and begin anew on a completely different track. Then, after a new completion, go through the evaluative process once more. And *again,* if necessary!

Exercise 5.1 *Following the procedure of simultaneous composition and description, write a one-part work in mixed (homophonic and polyphonic) styles. Evaluate.*

Exercise 5.2 *Write a work similar to that composed for Exercise 5.1, but with a different set of precompositional assumptions. Describe and evaluate.*

6. Composing a Two-Part Work: Song, Dance, Invention

A two-part work may be quite small, or it may be rather extended. The Trio of Beethoven's *Piano Sonata,* Op. 26, second movement, has but twenty-four measures;[1] the gavotte-like movement (without the "trio") of Prokofiev's *Classical Symphony*, only twelve, if one excludes the repetition of the last eight.[2] Larger binary forms appear in the second movement of Beethoven's *String Quartet in D major*, Op. 18, no. 3 (151 measures), and the finale of Mozart's *Concerto in D minor for Piano and Orchestra*, K. 466 (429 measures).[3]

As previously indicated, two-part form should not be confused with a one-part form that has two halves. Part one of a two-part form has a greater sense of completion and finality at its end than does the close of the first half of a one-part form. The evidence is usually found in such factors as modulation (in a tonal work) and the strength of the cadence (usually authentic rather than half-). At the midpoint of a two-part work, there is usually either a complete stop in the motion, or a retransition to part two. The former procedure, associated with a reprise of each part, is typical of the Baroque style; the latter, without the repetitions, of Classic and Romantic works.

Good examples of Baroque practice are found in dance movements of suites and partitas, and the sonatas by Domenico Scarlatti.[4] Illustrations of the Classic-Romantic sonatina form (exposition and recapitulation) are the Overture to *The Marriage of Figaro,* by Mozart, and the fourth movement of Brahms's *Symphony No. 1 in C minor.*[5]

We shall treat binary form differently in each of our three projects: song, dance, and

1. See *KMF,* Example 11.1.
2. See *KMF,* Exercise 5, page 105.
3. See *KMF,* examples 24.4 and 24.7.
4. See the discussion of Scarlatti's binary form in Ralph Kirkpatrick, *Domenico Scarlatti,* Princeton University Press, 1953.
5. See *KMF,* chapters 11 and 13 and examples 19.11, 20.2, 20.3, 24.1–24.4, and 25.5–25.7.

invention. In the vocal work, we decide to amplify the form by using an introduction, interlude, and coda. In the dance, we shall dispense with these extensions but repeat each of the two parts. And in the invention, there will be neither structural embellishments nor repetitions, but we shall try to have greater continuity at the midpoint than that achieved by the other two projects.

In order to focus attention on the contrasting approaches to binary design, we use the identical language in all three works: an artificial scale, E-F-G♭-A♯-B-C-D♭-E,[6] a modified Phrygian mode nicely suited for pandiatonicism.[7] This mode has no whole-steps, unlike major and minor modes, but there are an augmented second (D♭-E) and a doubly augmented second (G♭-A♯). There are an equal number of perfect fifths (E-B, F-C, and G♭-D♭) and tritones (E-A♯, F-B, and G♭-C). The consecutive half-steps (E-F-G♭ and A♯-B-C-D♭) provide two clusters and an asymmetrical, disjunct division of the heptatonic scale, in contrast to the familiar symmetry of the conjunct tetrachords in major mode (C-D-E-F and G-A-B-C). There are no tendency tones, with the possible exception of F, which may resolve to E as a vestige of the scale's Phrygian origin. Harmony is non-functional, although E may be used as tonic, B as dominant.

As text for our first project, we choose the brief Agnus Dei from the Latin Mass, using as a model the illustration (Example 25.7) in *KMF* from Bach's *Mass in B minor.*[8] Our dance will be a gigue, and the invention distantly related to the work shown in part in *KMF,* Example 18.3.

Now that we have, figuratively, packed our bags, we should plan our first itinerary in more detail before setting off. It is time for another table.

Table 6.1 *Precompositional considerations for a two-part vocal work.*

STYLE	Modified Phrygian scale, pandiatonic, polyphonic *and* homophonic.
MEDIUM	Four-part mixed chorus, a cappella (piano or organ may double).
MOTIVES	Four-note figure used at the opening.
LENGTH	With the structural appendages already decided upon, we need about 30 measures in 4/4 or ₵. Each main part about 8–10 mm.

(continued)

6. See *KMF,* Example 18.3, which uses this scale.
7. A style in which all notes of the diatonic system are equally capable of forming chords; by definition, there is no dissonance within the system.
8. As our "song" comes into focus, it turns out rather to be a choral work. As a reminder of our first thought, we may employ a solo voice somewhere. Sometimes the route is changed even before the excursion has begun.

Table 6.1 *continued*

MOOD, CHARACTER	Sacred, devotional.
TEMPO	Slow, about 𝅗𝅥 = 48.
RANGE, DYNAMICS	Largely *mf,* a few small changes; middle and low registers.
CLIMAX	A moderate one, in part two.
EXTRA-MUSICAL IDEAS	The text: *Agnus Dei qui tollis peccata mundi, miserere nobis.*
AUDIENCE	For church or concert use.

On second thought, we shall need the keyboard instrument (*without* the voices) for the introduction, interlude, and coda; but let's plan to have it double the voices when they come in. Repetition of words is allowable (again, see *KMF,* Example 25.7); the binary musical form need not be a reflection of the two-part structure of the text; it is well to remember which words naturally go together and where the accents fall. In *miserere,* the strongest accent is on the third syllable, with secondary accent on the first; the second and fourth syllables are equally weak. Accent may be created by register (high is stronger than low) and duration, as well as by situation in the measure (beats 1 and 3 generally strong, 2 and 4 weak). In syncopation, the weak beat is given greatest stress.

If one marches right through the text, the composition is over before one can properly begin. It is instructive to examine Bach's text setting in the *Mass in B minor* (not that one should necessarily do it the same way). The complete text is used in both of the two parts. The key opening words, *Agnus Dei,* appear only three times: once at the beginning of each part, and again at the point of return to the tonic key—a quasi-restatement at m. 31, in the second phrase of part two. (This suggestion of return after departure provides a basis for considering the movement as in incipient ternary form.)[9] These two words never appear twice in a row, unlike the subsequent words, which are frequently repeated.

The next four words are used either as a group or in the following combinations: *qui tollis peccata* or *peccata mundi.*

The words *miserere nobis* normally are not separated. They appear three times in a row in the middle of part one, and again (once) at the end of the part. In part two, *miserere nobis* appears only in five consecutive statements at the end—a very logical use of repetition to signal a close. An isolated *miserere,* without *nobis,* in mm. 37–38 may be the result of a process in which the notes were written before the word setting had been determined.

A moderate amount of melismatic procedure (setting a syllable to several pitches rather than to one) provides contrast, an expressive musical line, and a substitute for a single long note when accent is desired. Italics show the frequently accented and melismatically treated syllables in Bach's setting:

9. See *KMF,* pages 111–115, for explanation of this term.

A-gnus *De*-i qui *tol*-lis pec-*ca*-ta mun-di,
mi-se-*re*-re no-bis.

The reason for this detail is that it is important to consider the relative advantages of various alternatives. A similar study but with a quite different outcome in one's own composition may prove quite satisfactory.

Example 6.1 *Composing a two-part* Agnus Dei *for SATB chorus and organ.*

Over a tonic pedal, we write two streams of perfect intervals, in contrary motion, so as to introduce all the scale degrees before the chorus enters. Falling motion in the upper line is designed to prepare for the similar quasi-motivic idea in the treatment of the words and to suggest the accented *A-* and *De-*. We try throughout to avoid square rhythms, through the use of ties over the bar line and dotted notes.

The chorus derives its pitches from the organ (very useful, particularly if the idiom is unfamiliar). The organ then rests, so we may hear the pure sound of the voices. The reentry of the organ provides both rhythmic impetus (an anacrusis) and preparation for the next notes to be sung.

We complete the first verbal phrase in the soprano using the same scale degrees (F, G♭, A♯, D♭) in a different arrangement; for ease in reading we write B♭ instead of A♯. More animated rhythm propels the music forward. As in mm. 4–6, the alto line follows the soprano a perfect interval below, with some passing tones in m. 8.

The tenor resembles the soprano in contour, is linked with the bass line in perfect intervals (like the two upper voices), and continues the method of mm. 4–6.

Unlike those measures, the lines form an arch that is associated with a rise and fall in the dynamics.

The organ largely doubles the voices. There is a growing sense of polyphony because of the several departures from rhythmic unison.

With the closing words, let us fulfill the promise of polyphony with some imitative entries. These heighten the tension and permit a sense of resolution in m. 12.

For additional contrast, we abandon the parallel perfect intervals to some degree in mm. 10–11 (note the calculated C-G♭ entries and the sustained E-B♭). The lower voices begin rather roughly, with emphasis on C-B. The final chord, composed of two perfect intervals, B-G♭ (=F♯) and C-F, is relatively restful. The long notes, *piano*, and linear termination assist the realization of cadence.

More is needed, to create a stronger cadence for part one. This is accomplished by the bass solo in mm. 13–15, with supporting bass line in the organ. We end in unison on the dominant, B.

Following the cadence, we write an instrumental interlude, as planned. Continuing the imitative style just introduced, we thicken the texture to four voices in the organ, using a four-note motive based upon the rhythm ♩ ♩ | ♩ ♩ , which derives from both "*A*-gnus *De*-i" and "*mi*-se-*re*-re." The line usually descends, in keeping with the sentiment of the text.

First to be written is the soprano line, mm. 15–17, which omits the tonic E. The tenor line imitates at the tritone, with a change of imitation interval to avoid octave doubling. The alto has a fragment, related to the soprano line, in inversion.

The last three measures are imitative, using a variant of the motive. The pedal line augments the motive, to suggest tempo broadening.

Part two of a binary structure is seldom shorter than part one. But we decide to try it, and hope to make it "work" by using compression and overlap.

The first half of part two stresses the interval of a third and triadic groups. The overall mood is more tranquil in its prayer for mercy. The texture involves simultaneous (parallel) rhythms in the three upper voices. The basses, already distinguished by the solo in mm. 13–15, mournfully intone the same notes (C-B) they had in mm. 11–12, in augmentation.

The notes in the upper lines were secured after it was determined which scale degrees might be used. There are only four possible consonant thirds (C-E, D♭-F, B♭ (A♯)-D, and G♭-B♭ (A♯). We found two possible major triads and one dominant-seventh.

A half-cadence in E is suggested in m. 27, but the music moves, surprisingly, to B♭ (enharmonic leading tone of the dominant).

The second half of part two uses as text only the last two words. The music is a modified transposition of mm. 10–15, and provides the terminal parallelism with part one that is a characteristic of binary form.[10]

The basses continue their solitary and non-imitative path, with octave doubling to provide additional sonority.

The three-measure codetta in the organ overlaps the end of the choral parts by one measure. The material is derived from mm. 13–15. We redirect it so that it ends securely, and with sufficient duration, on the tonic, E, instead of on the dominant.

10. This is a significant distinction from *period* form, where the parallelism tends to be at the beginning.

Evaluating our work, we note that the tempo was changed from MM. 60 to MM. 48, which probably helps to achieve the devotional mood. The motivic elements proved to be somewhat different than originally conceived: the falling second and the perfect interval (usually descending) appear with sufficient frequency to be regarded as equally motivic. The single use of bass solo is perhaps not as satisfactory as multiple use, and at least a short second solo might be worked in, should a revision ensue. The terminal compression results in a conclusion that is satisfactory but, to these ears, is a bit short. A compensatingly longer coda would probably provide a better result.

Our second project is the gigue, and we begin by preparing our list of limiting factors.

Table 6.2 *Precompositional considerations for a two-part dance work ("Gigue").*

STYLE	Same as for Example 6.1.
MEDIUM	Two flutes and cello.
LENGTH	32 measures (16+16, with each part repeated).
MOOD, CHARACTER	Lively.
TEMPO, METER	♩. = 108 in 6/8.
RANGE, DYNAMICS	Largely in middle range; *piano* with occasional *forte* passages.
CLIMAX	Moderate, in part two.
EXTRA-MUSICAL IDEAS	None, except for the dance element.
AUDIENCE	Concert, or as a dance recital piece.
MOTIVES	[rhythmic motive], involving steps or leaps. The inversion is favored in part two, following Baroque-era practice.

Apart from drawing our bar lines, we should now plan the subdivisions. Since dances frequently, and for practical reason, use symmetrical groupings, each 16 will be 4 × 4, with each four consistent in the treatment of materials and slightly contrasting with its neighbors. The precise nature of these consistencies and contrasts will be determined as we move along.

At this point, we deliberately limit the range of possibilities in order not to have to work within an inordinate range of alternatives, with the understanding that as the work progresses, new horizons present new challenges and opportunities for exploration and discovery. With this in mind, we draw our bar lines and begin to sketch.

Example 6.2 *Composing a two-part gigue.*

We write the important bass line first. The repeated tonic establishes the key; stepwise motion to B demonstrates the scale and mode as well as the dominant. The bass in mm. 5–8 is a modified inversion, also ending on B (as "V" in E).

Flutes are imitative at the octave. Flute 2 begins almost as a decorated doubling of the cello line, to permit a more diversified texture when it is needed later. We are careful, otherwise, to avoid octave doubling in general. The motive is varied for mm. 5–8, to help clarify the 4+4 phrase structure.

The climax is reached relatively early (m. 5), following which the line gradually descends.

It is time to prepare for the end of part one. Again, we compose the bass line first, carefully approaching B and permitting its repetition (cadential extension?) to m. 16. For the first time, the cello engages in brief motivic interplay with the upper lines. A few accents and brief *forte* create new tension, to heighten the following sense of repose. The texture thins out; repeated B's in the flute phrases assist in the cadence. One hopes that this helps to clarify material and the form. The repeated notes at the beginning take on new significance, because of the similar treatment in mm. 13–16.

For part two, we decide to use in inversion the material that opened part one—common practice in the Baroque gigue. The bass line and the upper voices reflect this decision for a few measures, but quickly depart from it. In mm. 19–22, the cello has a 2+2 sequence, ascending, during which flute 2 crosses it for the first time, in a crescendo. We decide, again, to have an early climax (m. 23). The repeated dotted quarters appear, somewhat motivically. We should develop our ideas somewhat, and so permit the cello to play arco as well as pizzicato and engage in further imita-

tion of the flutes; contrast, for them, is provided by a few long notes, use of the repeated tone (m. 22) and hemiola (mm. 26–29). The subdivisions, 4+4+4+4, disappear, but the closing three-bar group clearly resembles the four-bar group that concludes part one. To make this possible, we worked backward from the double bar.

In a few respects, our trio resembles the trio sonata style of the Baroque era, because of the pairing of the two upper lines and the contrasting, accompanimental nature of the bass line. In contrast to part one, which displays inner balance and symmetry, part two is a bit "unruly." Its balances are asymmetrical and therefore more unpredictable and more commanding of attention. Imitation is often associated with overlapping measure groups. Hemiola, as used here, is largely a product of augmentation (where becomes) and is not at all arbitrary.

Critical evaluation might take us to task for writing so conservative a work, based as it is on an old style. But there are things to be learned from this "exercise," and (as Prokofiev showed in the *Classical Symphony*) possibly the "old bottles" still are congenial to "new wine". Additional criticism might be directed at the attempt to borrow tonic and dominant functions from major and minor modes, at the beginnings and endings, when harmonic functions are otherwise absent. Again, this manner of combining functional and non-functional harmonies, although it appears an inconsistency, resembles the use of chromaticism within the larger framework of diatonicism in composers from Bach to Wagner and Franck.[11] Our use of the motive is rather moderate, not insistent, with more employment of fragments than of the motive as a whole. The enharmonic equivalents here and there may be a bit confusing at first,

11. See *KMT*, Volume 2, Chapter 23.

but for the performer they are an aid in sight-reading. Perhaps, for a contemporary work, use of special effects (flutter-tongue or fingering the keys without blowing, in the flutes, for example) might have given the work a more "up-to-date" sound. Such criticism, however, would be more valid if we had indicated our preliminary intention to use such devices.

Our third study using the altered Phrygian mode is to be an invention in style. We reduce the texture further, to two *voices.* The medium: piano or harpsichord (the latter lends itself particularly well to this thin texture). The two *parts* will be distinguished more by the way we use the motives than by separation (as in Example 6.1) or by double reprise and strong cadences at ends of parts (see Example 6.2). As appropriate to invention style, we shall adhere more closely to the motives as defined, considerably limiting the degree of admissible variation. The interest should derive from the way we are able to devise effective means of developing our ideas within the strict, self-imposed limitations.

Table 6.3 *Precompositional considerations for a two-part (two-section) invention in two voices.*

STYLE	Same scale, key, and mode as used in the prior examples.
MEDIUM	Piano or harpsichord.
LENGTH	About 40–50 measures.
TEMPO, METER	Very fast, in 7/8; subdivisions variable, but chiefly 2+2+3.
MOTIVES	Several rhythmic-melodic ideas: *a*)  , its inversion  ; *b*) a scalar variant  and its inversion  ; plus purely rhythmic motives *c*) ; *d*)  ; and *e*)  , in which it will be noted that *c* is an unequal division of the measure; *d* is an augmentation of seven eighth-notes; and *e* is an even division of the measure.
MOOD, CHARACTER	Light, playful, sometimes playfully threatening.
CLIMAX	Very near the end.
AUDIENCE	Concert (encore piece?)

Our next step, in the interest of efficiency, is the planning of subdivisions—their length and the contents that will distinguish each unit from its neighbor. (The reader who still regards this as too cold-blooded and calculated is reminded that these limitations are self-imposed and that, if they are excessively constricting, they may be removed or revised.) Part one, this time, shall be a bit shorter than part two, and the latter is to be followed by a codetta; respective lengths: twenty, twenty-four, four (total forty-eight).

Part one is to be subdivided in turn, so as to form an arithmetic progression, 2+3+4+5+6 (=20), and part two, a reverse arithmetic progression, 9+8+7 (=24). We thus have a modified mirror procedure, designed to avoid repetition of symmetrical measure groups and to achieve the greatest intensity in the middle of the work by virtue of the longer units—short units being best suited for initial announcements and concluding formalities (the "hellos" and "goodbyes" of music).

We decide to introduce all the motives in part one, with each of the five small subdivisions favoring one of the motives primarily, whereas part two will be more developmental, in that motives are heard more in counterpoint against each other—there is more double counterpoint, which is a sort of trademark of invention style.

In our commentary, we shall refer to inversions of *a* and *b* as a^1 and b^1, respectively. Motive *c* can be "inverted" only in the sense of retrograde, and that alteration we shall identify as c^1. Motives *d* and *e* are, of course, not invertible.

The scalar variants will of necessity have different contours because of the peculiarities of the mode we are using.[12] This should be regarded as a special asset of this mode, an opportunity for varied repetition, not available in such marked degree in major and minor and, obviously, completely unavailable in a chromatic or a whole-tone scale.

Example 6.3 *Composing a two-part invention for piano or harpsichord.*

We unfold the 2+3+4+5+6 as follows: upper line presents motives *a* and *c* in mm. 1–2; lower voice imitates at the octave in mm. 3–4, and m. 5 is an extension by sequence in both voices. The four-measure unit (mm. 6–9) consists of 2+2 with further use of motives *a* and *c*, and the new element of parallelism in mm. 6 and 8.

12. G♭-A♯-B-C-D♭-E-F-G♭ has the large intervals in different places, for example, than the scale beginning one step higher.

The five-measure unit (mm. 10–14) grows out of m. 9 almost imperceptibly: the unity of the group is established by consistent use of double counterpoint of motives *b* and *c* (or c^1)—motive *a* is not used here. A gradual climax to the high notes, *forte*, is developed in these measures.

Mm. 15–20 have the "responsibility" of cadencing in an area other than E. In contrast to Examples 6.1 and 6.2, part one ends on the tritone, B♭ (not B). Motives *b*, *d*, and *e* appear in a descending line, with double counterpoint in mm. 15–18.

After the cadence, weakened by continuing motion, we attempt to clarify the beginning of part two by making sudden changes in dynamics and tessitura, and by dropping the upper voice for one measure.

The opening nine-measure group is unified by imitative treatment of motive *a* in augmentation, linking it thus with *d*. In counterpoint with it are *un*augmented *a*, and *doubly* augment-

ed *a*, which is linked with *c*. Use of middle register in mm. 23–25 suggests a third voice. Motive *a* is treated canonically, as a stretto, in mm. 27–29. The many overlapping groups help ensure the nine-measure continuum, which we deliberately break at m. 30 by means of dynamic and tessitura change, with the *Luftpause* (′) or pause for breath, as an assist.

The eight-measure group features contrary motion; rhythms are either identical (mm. 30–31, 34–35) or staggered (mm. 32–33, 36–37). Unity in mm. 30–37 is achieved through repetition (m. 31 is an octave transposition of m. 30) and sequence (mm. 32–33). The entire eight is 4+4, thanks to our decision to make mm. 34–37 a repetition of 30–33, somewhat disguised by the use of double counterpoint and the crescendo.

What better way to fill seven measures (38–44) than a *triple* augmentation of motive *a*, with one measure for each note? To separate this section further from its neighbors, we use *a* twice in fragmented form, in the upper voice, followed by its inversion. Rests make it possible for the one-measure figure to occupy two measures. Asymmetrical entries accentuate the sense of coming apart.[13]

A four-measure coda is largely a settling down on the tonic, with octave doubling at the close.

An objective description of the invention might include the following observations: the rather insistent eighths suggest a sort of perpetual-motion machine, which, of course, tends to characterize the Baroque use of this style. On the other hand, there is more dramatic contrast here than in the Bach models, where dynamics are not given. Some of the demands on the performer are considerable, especially in matters of rhythm. The mode is possibly a bit wearisome without any chromatic variants, but this may be no problem in a work of such brief duration. The two parts are clear enough, but one might question here the distinction between two-part form and a one-part form with two halves, since the matter of mid point cadence in a different key is ambiguous. The work is rather better suited to the piano than to the harpsichord for a variety of reasons, among them the crescendos and diminuendos (impossible on the harpsichord) and the very large number of dynamic levels. A somewhat different version for harpsichord, with registration and reworking of the dynamics, might be effective. The reader may have additional observations and critical evaluations.

13. See a similar procedure in Beethoven's *Symphony No. 3 in E♭* ("Eroica"), end of second movement.

Exercise 6.1 *Make several precompositional plans for a variety of two-part compositions, using tables 6.1, 6.2, and 6.3 as models. Each proposed work should treat binary form differently and be for a different performance medium. Make the details as complete as possible.*

Exercise 6.2 *Following approval of one or more of the plans, commence work on the compositions, providing comments on your thought processes and decisions in the manner of examples 6.1, 6.2, and 6.3.*

Exercise 6.3 *Following completion of all or a part of your work, write an objective evaluation and a critique as if the work were viewed by someone other than yourself. Revise and polish as needed. If wholesale revision is needed, scrap the sketches and begin over—but it is well, in this case, to understand clearly the reasons for lack of success, in order to minimize the possibility of repeating the same non-productive procedures. Lack of inspiration (whatever that may be) is probably* not *the problem. The best way to find inspiration is to play with the possibilities and then, having found a satisfying and pleasing choice, use the emotion of satisfaction as a platform for launching your next step, and so on. In short, inspiration is derived from the pleasure of satisfactorily accomplished work—it does not precede the work.*

7. Composing a Three-Part Work: Song, Dance, Invention; Transition, Retransition, Introduction, Extension

As there are various types of small binary form, so there are different kinds of ternary form.[1] The term usually refers to the design *aba,* not *abc;* the former consists of a statement, a departure, and a return (exact or modified); the latter is more properly an open, through-composed form; *aba* is a "closed form," like a circle, whereas *abc* is more a straight line or an arch.

Basic questions in the *aba* design plan include the following: 1) Is a^2 (the second *a*) an exact or a modified restatement of a^1 (the first *a*)? 2) If modified, what are the changes in general and in detail? 3) What is the relationship of *b* to a^1 in material, treatment, length, and so on? 4) What is the key scheme of a^1? of *b*? of a^2? and what types of cadence are used at the ends of these parts? 5) Does our design include the formal repetition of a^1 and of ba^2, as in the Classic-era menuetto (or scherzo) and trio?[2] 6) Will the retransition from *b* to a^2 be integral to *b* or contrasting in texture, possibly an anticipation of elements of a^2? 7) Will there be any expansions of the form by means of an introduction or codetta?[3]

Since these questions should be answered in any and all tables of precompositional considerations, we need not list them in the following pages. But we shall mention them in our running comments that parallel the composition of each work.

Each of our three projects should display a different aspect of three-part design. Our song will be *aba* without repeats but with introduction, retransition, and coda. The dance piece, following Classic precedent, will have neither introduction nor coda, but a retransition will lead us from *b* to a^2, and there will be a double reprise (a^1 and ba^2 are repeated). For contrast,

1. See *KMF,* chapters 12, 13, and 14.
2. See *KMF,* examples 14.1 (diagrams) and 14.2 (music and diagrams).
3. See *KMF,* Example 14.4, particularly the Trio, which has extensions at the ends of the first and third parts of the ternary form.

we plan for the invention to have an *abc* design with two transitions, one at the end of *a*, the other at the end of *b*.

In the first work (the *aba* song) the *a* parts will be almost if not exactly identical,[4] the retransition an outgrowth of *b*. In the second work, a scherzo, a^2 will be longer than a^1 and stay in the tonic key rather than modulate, as a^1 does; the retransition will anticipate elements of a^2. The third work will have cadences in non-tonic areas near the ends of *a* and *b*, followed by dissolving transitions; a strong tonic cadence at the end of *c*; and no retransitions.[5]

To unify our study further, we shall write each work for a different solo with piano accompaniment. The song is for high voice (soprano or tenor), the scherzo for violin, the invention for flute.

Extending our twentieth-century techniques, we experiment with bitonal combinations. The number of common tones varies; thus, if one writes in C and G, all are common tones except F and F♯, with little contrast; but if the music is in C and F♯, then only F (E♯) and B are common tones (considerable contrast). To secure complete absence of common tones, one might use either mutually exclusive pentatonic (C-D-E-G-A vs. D♭-E♭-G♭-A♭-B♭) or whole-tone scales (C-D-E-F♯-G♯ vs. D♭-E♭-F-G-A-B).

The author confesses to a fondness for near-nonsense texts, such as those by Lewis Carroll; for texts that, to an outsider, border on the absurd, such as the directions for disassembly of an automatic pistol as given in an army manual (set to music by the author during his military service); and for the existential absurdities to be found in such writers as Ionesco and the Kafka of *Amerika* and *Metamorphosis* (the author has written a three-act opera based upon the former). So it was natural enough to seek out similar material for our song. It was tempting to use one of the shorter poems in *Alice in Wonderland*, such as "The Lobster Quadrille," which has three stanzas, but that piece lends itself better to strophic setting. Somewhat closer in spirit to Milhaud's song setting of a seed catalog is our final choice: excerpts from a bridge game as described in a daily newspaper. To a person unfamiliar with the game, the words add up to something akin to impressionistic prose, almost an abstraction. Each of the four sides, North, East, South, West, should be represented, it seemed to us. But in what order should they appear, and how should they fit into the procrustean bed of ternary form we have prepared in advance? Our solution began with an examination of the lines to determine which would be best suited to match (as a^1 and a^2), which one would best serve as contrasting middle, and which one be suitable for the coda. The "prose," if one may call it that, had to be metricized, and the *a* sections thought out, so that the different rhythms of each could somehow be brought into unison or compromise. We provide, first, the four sentences extracted from the original five paragraphs; second, our procedure in metricizing and bringing to agreement the texts to be used in a^1 and a^2. Only then do we make some musical decisions.

4. For precedent, see *KMF*, examples 12.1 and 25.9. In 25.10, parts one and three are identical but for the closing cadences.
5. For retransitions that are outgrowths of *preceding* sections, see *KMF*, Example 13.9 (Interlude 3); that are anticipatory of *next* section, *KMF*, Example 13.7; that are *contrasting* in texture and material, *KMF*, Example 14.2. The middle sections in *KMF*, Example 14.4, have *no* retransitions but end, rather, on half-cadences (see mm. 25–26 and 73–74).

Example 7.1 *Composing a song ("The Card Game") in ternary form.*

First step: Select the four lines needed for the *aba*+coda form, and put them in logical order.

> *West* had no clear-cut lead, and led a trump in the hope that this would give nothing away.
>
> *North's* response of two hearts was a transfer, promising at least five cards in spades.
>
> *East* should now have realized that his fine collection of cards was deceptive.
>
> *South* put up the queen, which was allowed to win.[6]

Although selected out of original sequence, some sense of logic is apparent in the leading action of West, a response by North, the thoughtfulness of East, and the triumph of South.

Second step: Iron out the differences between West and East. To do this, we vertically aligned the two texts, and put in tentative "bar lines" to show where the accented syllables fall. Obviously, some accommodation will be necessary in one part or the other, with the shorter line becoming a bit stretched in order not to get ahead of its companion. The result of this process may be seen as:

(1)	(2)	(3)	(4)	(5)
West had	no	clear-cut	lead, and	led a
East should	now have	re - a -	lized that	(𝄽) his

(6)	(7)	(8)	(9)	(10)
trump	in the	hope that	this	would give
fine col-	lec -	tion of	high	cards was de-

(11)	(12)
no-thing a-	way.
cep -	tive.

A few measures need special attention. In m. 5, "that" may be tied over from m. 4, replacing the rest. In m. 10, we will possibly need a triplet in the lower line against two beats above. The last two measures pose the greatest problem, because the upper line ends with an accent, the lower with a weak pulse. One solution of the problem is to rework the end of the second line as follows: "/ cards / was de- / cep-tive /." If not ideal, at least it is an improvement (*-tive* is now more unaccented).

Third step: Work out the precise relative durations for each "measure" (or metrical foot) for a^1 and a^2, showing also the internal breathing points, which should appear at the same place for both lines (we show these here by dotted line). After trying and rejecting 𝄵 and 2/4 we settled, finally, on 3/4.

6. Text from Alan Truscott's "Bridge" column, *International Herald Tribune,* April 28, 1978. Used by permission.

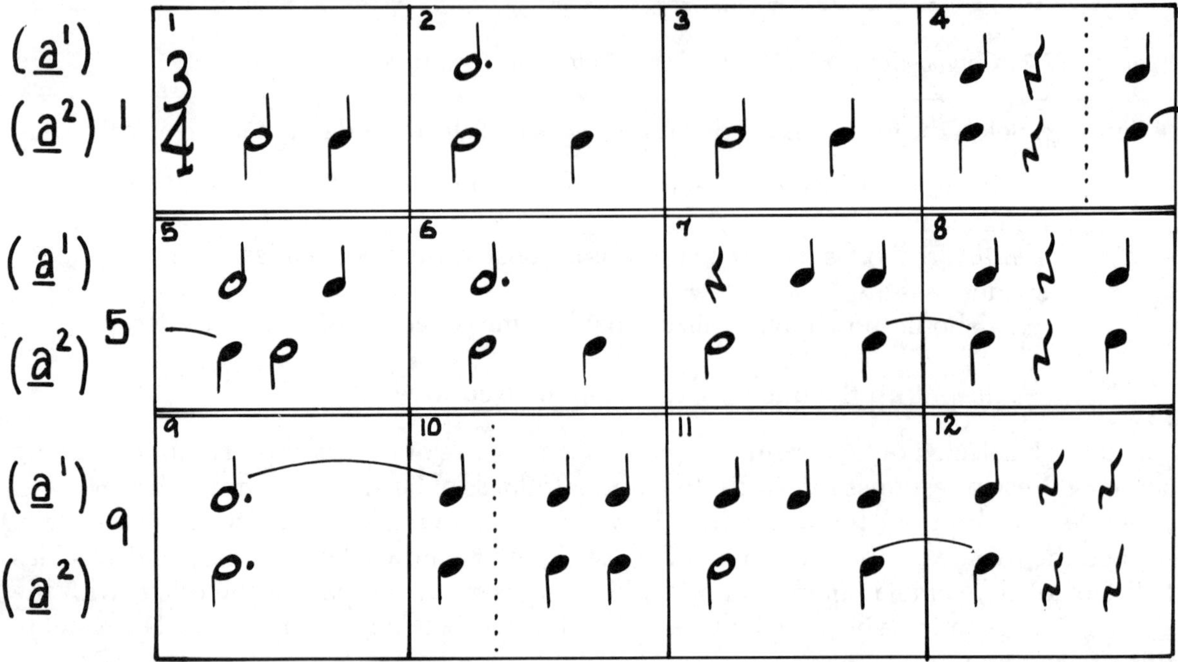

Fourth step: Work out a melodic line that will accommodate *both* rhythmic schemes, using the given text. To achieve maximum effect of dry humor, we choose the two keys of C and F♯ because they have the fewest common tones and therefore suggest the greatest degree of absurdity. We decide to permit the voice to use all the twelve tones. The piano accompaniment, when it is written, should support the vocal line but at the same time use one key for the right-hand part, the other key for the left-hand part.

The thinking behind the choice of notes included the following considerations. The *range* was decided as e^1 to e♭², a comfortable middle-register octave. The (high) E♭ was the logical *climax* note, and, fortuitously, it could be used for the word "high" and also for the word "this," which is vocally suited to a high pitch. The *nadir,* our lowest pitch, would appear at the end, appropriate for a cadence and for the final syllables "-way" and "-tive." The next-highest and next-lowest tones will be adjacent to the climax and nadir, permitting them to be approached by step rather than by the vocally more awkward leap. We then decided that the climax should be approached by ascending steps, using notes not already sounded. The opening four measures (2+2) seemed to suggest a rising sequence, hence the two ascending thirds.

Only mm. 1 and 3 have identical notes in the two lines. Differences in the others are minimal and do not seriously jeopardize our plan to have a^2 a repetition of a^1. We made the changes in the interest of clarity and naturalness of expression in the singing of the words. Forced agreement would be arbitrary, inartistic, and unjustifiable. A different accommodation is quite possible—what is important here is the *method* and the nature of the problem to be solved.

We leave for last the introduction, retransition, and coda. Steps five and six involve working out the accompaniment for a^1 (which will serve a^2 as well), and all of *b* (in which we again work out the vocal line first, then the accompaniment).

Fifth step: We work out a bitonal accompaniment, with C major for the left-hand part, G♭ (=F♯) major for the right-hand part. Tempo: a fast three. Mood: sardonic, humorous, dry. A few sudden dynamic changes for brief "shock" effect. Texture: homophonic, with broken chords, occasional short scale runs. Mild dissonances only. We prepare the score by putting in the bar lines, and write the vocal line for a^1 above the still-empty measures of the piano part.

After one unsatisfactory start that seemed too meandering, we hit upon the following plan for the texture and harmonies in the accompaniment: to prevent the competition of other melodic lines, we limit ourselves to chord outlines; the chords must support the given melody, and retain their tritone relationship throughout. Our first thoughts, after that, were of suitable root progressions, bass line, avoidance of undue repetition, motivic ideas, rhythmic counterpoint in the broken chords, preparation for and realization of the climax at the word "this," and cadence in the closing measures. After writing the music we discovered that we had used the following harmonic scheme, *in both keys simultaneously:*

I-I-V-I, III-VI-III-III, IV-II-V-I.

With one chord per measure (except for mm. 1–2 and 7–8, which prolong I and III, respectively), the harmonic rhythm is clear and consistent. The first four establish the keys; the next four center on the mediant; the last four are cadential. The logic of the harmonic progression provides a good foil for the whimsy of the text and the bitonal arrangement. This is how it turned out:

The two motives used in the first measure continue through the twelve measures, with variation to ensure interest and to help support the meaning of the words. The text implies a rather sly, deliberately misleading action on the part of "West," hence the displaced accents in the last four measures and the surprising rest on the first beat of the ninth measure.

Sixth step: We compose the middle part, *b*, keeping in mind that it will be followed by an instrumental retransition that leads the music to a^2. Once again, melody first, then the accompaniment. Before we put notes on paper, metric and rhythmic elements should be determined—then we can supply pitches. Some contrast, but not too much, is desirable for this part.

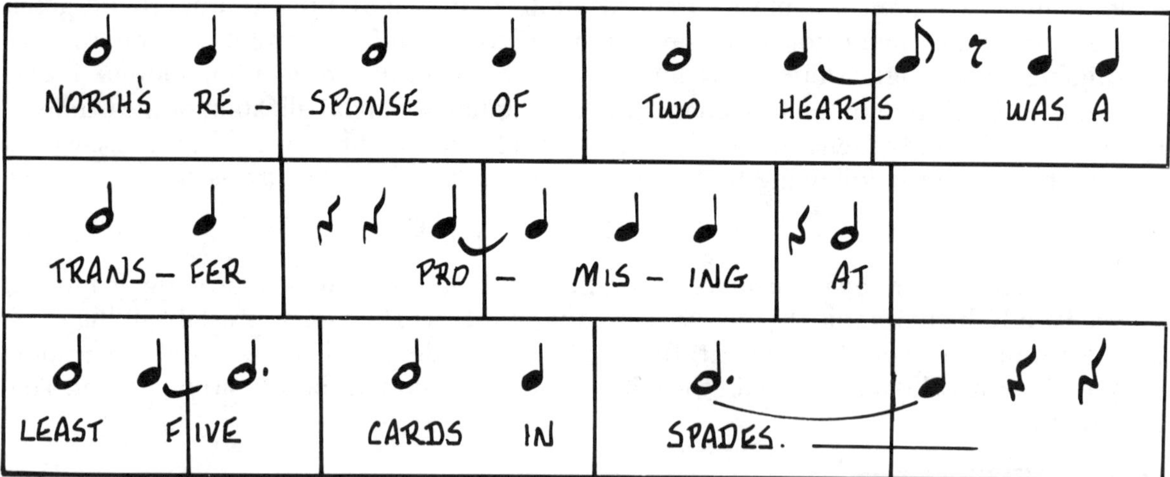

By happy chance, we find it necessary to have considerable contrast between the meter and the rhythm, hence the hemiola in mm. 3–4 and several ties over the bar line. Rather than provide the words "least five cards" with equal accents, we shorten "least" and lengthen "five," which is the climax and also a nice open sound for the voice. In m. 8, we gave "at" two beats instead of one, to provide a further suggestion of 2/4 against the underlying 3/4 meter. The number of measures turns out to be twelve once again—but with the retransition added, *b* will be longer than a^1.

We decide to raise the tessitura by a whole step (the climax will be F instead of D♯/E♭), and to reverse the keys in the piano part (C major will be in the upper rather than the lower register). As in a^1, each measure uses a different one of the twelve tones; we choose the climax and nadir tones first, and always consider the suitability of high and low notes for the vowel sounds with which they are to be associated.

We decide to balance the higher climax in *b* with the use of three falling melodic groups, as follows:

Scale degrees:	G♭	G	A♭	A	B♭	B	C	D♭	D	E♭	E	F
Measure number:	5	2	4	1	3	9	8	7	6	12	11	10

These were found by working back from the end (and climax), 12-11-10, the highest note being in m. 10, using chromatic half-steps. The next four measures (6-7-8-9) went similarly in reverse, so the two groups (6–9 and 10–12) have a somewhat sequential relationship. The other group of measures (1–5) also is planned in retrograde order, but with the pitches staggered (A-G and B♭-A♭-G♭), so as to secure a contrasting "diatonic" set of progressions. If we now combine words, rhythms, and pitch successions, we secure the following line:

Unlike a^1, *b* has no comma in the text. But the break after "transfer" is logical, and both the leap and the rests assist in the caesura. The style is similar to *a*, as is customary in the *b* part of a small part-form, but the substance is sufficiently different to provide the desired contrast. The falling seconds in mm. 1–4 turn out to be varied inversions of the rising thirds in the same measures of a^1, a happy coincidence and an example of the variation principle—and perhaps of the subconscious mind at work. We are ready now to add the accompaniment. Only the harmonic design needs to be determined. Here it is: three four-measure groups.

$$\left.\begin{matrix}\text{C:}\\ \text{F}\sharp\text{:}\end{matrix}\right\}\ V^{9}\text{-I-I-}V_{\binom{6}{4}},\ \text{VI-II-V-}I_{\binom{6}{4}},\ V_{\substack{6\\5}}\text{-}V^{7}\text{-VI-IV}\ldots$$

Clearly there is no cadence, but rather a dissolution prior to the return to *a*. The keys have exchanged position, somewhat in the manner of double counterpoint.

Seventh step: We now write the retransition, which we decided would grow out of b in substance while leading us linearly to a^2. Six measures should be enough. And a^2 is so prepared that we can write it without further ado.

The retransition should be planned with the bass line or the harmonies (or both) in mind. A postcadential extension (by repetition, or continuation) may dissolve into the next part.[7]

7. See *KMF*, Example 21.5, mm. 23–29 and diagram (page 228), and Example 12.3 with diagram (page 109).

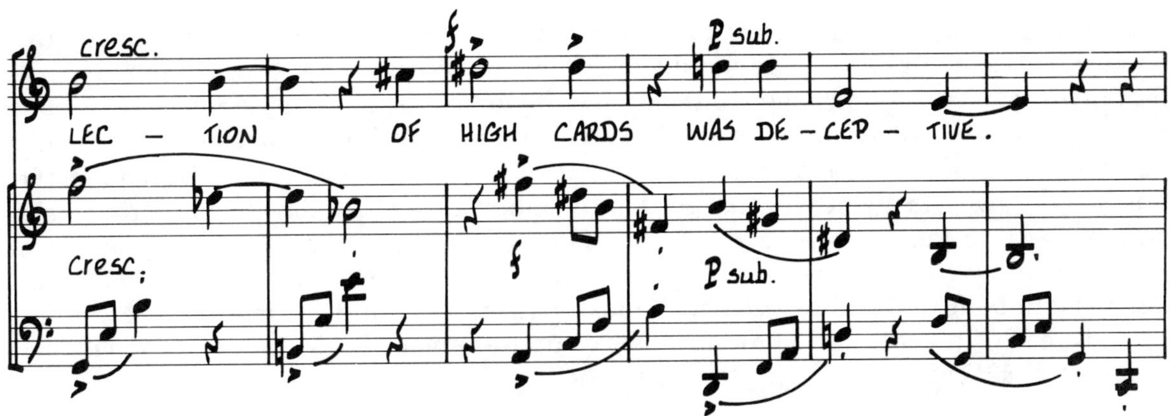

We made a few alterations of rhythm in the melody line to improve the balance of durations in certain vowels. Thus, more emphasis was given the words "fine" and "should," and equal emphasis was given to "high" and "cards." The retransition actually uses materials (the triad outline in eighths and the one using quarters) of both *a* and *b*, and thus is an anticipation of a^2 as well as an outgrowth of *b*.

Eighth and ninth steps: Composition of the coda and the introduction. We decide to adapt the last six measures of *a* for the introduction, since they help establish the keys and overall style, and take elements of the retransition for the coda. The retransition recrosses the tonalities (so that G♭/F♯ is once again above, C below); but in the coda, C is already below, so the exchange will not take place during the postcadential extension—in its place we will endeavor to prolong the harmonies, and provide for the voice a quasi-recitativo that will make clear that it is not providing a part four.

Tenth step: Assembly of all the parts and examination of the connections to be sure there is good articulation. A performance should determine the success of our efforts. Comedy, in its best manifestations, is much more difficult to write than tragedy or the serious, and is often rather unjustly regarded as a lesser art. The reverse side of this coin is that solemnity is often mistaken for profundity, and when it is combined with unintelligibility is likely to inspire undeserved awe and reverence. This peculiarity, more noticeable today than in earlier times, may go back to the dawn of civilization, when only an inner circle of high priests was assumed to have knowledge of the eternal verities, and mysterious incantations were a language to be feared and respected. We take passing note of three masterpieces of high comedy, each different, each a product of the composer's maturity: Mozart's *The Magic Flute*, Wagner's *Die Meistersinger*, and Verdi's *Falstaff*.

Example 7.2 *Composing a scherzo in ternary form.*

First step: Select the meter and the chief motive. We decide on a quick 5/4 and the motive | 𝅗𝅥 𝅗𝅥 𝅘𝅥 |, with variants 𝅘𝅥 | 𝅗𝅥 𝅗𝅥 and | 𝅘𝅥 𝅘𝅥 𝅘𝅥 𝅘𝅥 𝅘𝅥 |. Then the major scales, to be used bitonally as in Example 7.1. The less contrasting major scales of C and E are chosen—providing several common tones (E, A, and B—the I, IV, and V in E major). Between the two keys, all twelve tones are available except B♭(A♯).

Second step: Make a diagram of the proposed form showing the three parts, the retransition, the double reprise, and the overall harmonic scheme. The solo violin may participate in both keys, but in general the piano right hand is in E, the left hand in C. This repeats the arbitrary but useful plan we employed in Example 7.1. The key with sharps is *above* the key with no signature, to provide a brighter result from an acoustical point of view.

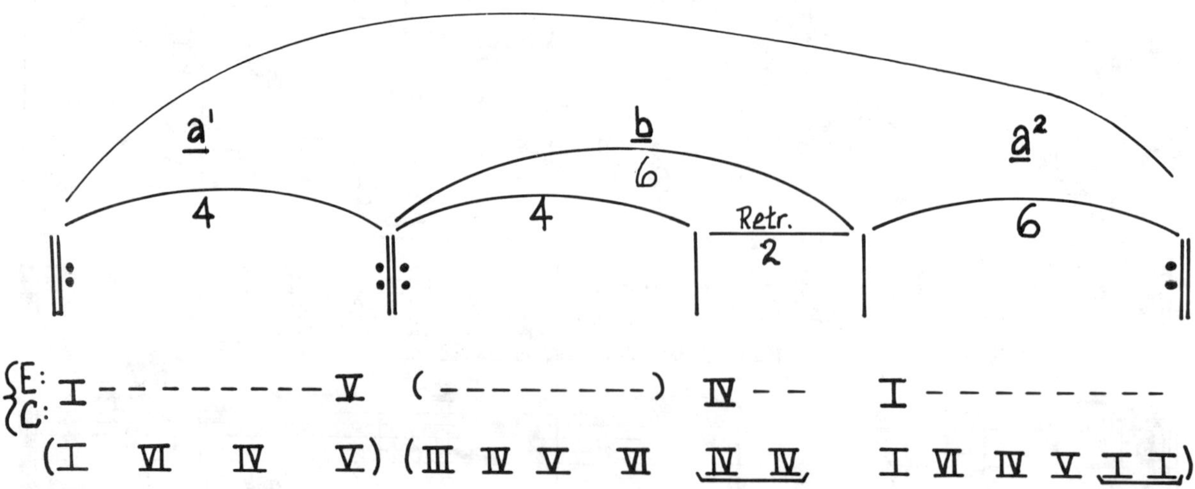

Third step: Plan the harmonic details within the larger framework already established. In a^1, we shall endeavor to have a homophonic texture; in *b*, a polyphonic, with a mixture of the two in a^2. This procedure helps to ensure increasing interest and tension. Material in the retransition should suggest (by anticipation) the return of *a,* and lead into it stepwise. The prolongation of the tonic at the end of a^2 should provide the stability needed at that point.

Fourth step: Write the violin part first, then the piano accompaniment. Choose the notes in accordance with the chosen chords.

In the violin part, we tried to use both keys alternatively. Thus, in m. 1, E and B belong to E major; C, G, and E to C major. In m. 2, the order is reversed, first two notes in C, then three in E. In general, the notes involve motion between the *preestablished* chord tones. The two tritones of m. 4 represent the critical notes of the V^7-chord in E and C respectively, while the piano provides the complete chords.

In *b,* the close imitation (after two beats) tends to weaken the sense of the meter. The previously unused running eighths in m. 8 provide contrast and are used corroboratively in mm. 9 and 14. (This is a good principle to remember—anything worth doing once should be repeated at least once.) The climax is reached in the retransition. A brief ritenuto helps prepare the listener for the return at m. 11.

In a^2, the melody of a^1, originally in the violin only, is treated in turn in the violin, piano right-hand, and piano left-hand parts. M. 14, although corresponding to m. 4, has new, active material in the piano part. The last two measures have no counterpart in a^1 and combine material from both a^1 and *b,* including the close imitation, now at the distance of only one beat; harmonically, they provide a settling on the two tonic chords. The final beat is a sort of hiccup, derived from the sforzandos on the fifth beats of mm. 1–3.

The intertwining and overlapping of materials and procedures is designed to exhaust fairly well the potentials of what has been begun. Nevertheless, this scherzo might well serve as part of a larger movement (scherzo-trio-scherzo da capo) to provide the opportunity to hear again the rather intricate minutiae, which move on rather quickly at scherzo tempo.

For our invention, three keys are used, A♭, C, and E major, to secure considerable contrast. The octave is divided into three equal parts—each segment is a major third or the enharmonic equivalent, similar to the augmented triad in interval components. There is a single motive, indicated below, that is used in inversion, stretto, and augmentation.

The motive (x):

The motive used imitatively in three keys:

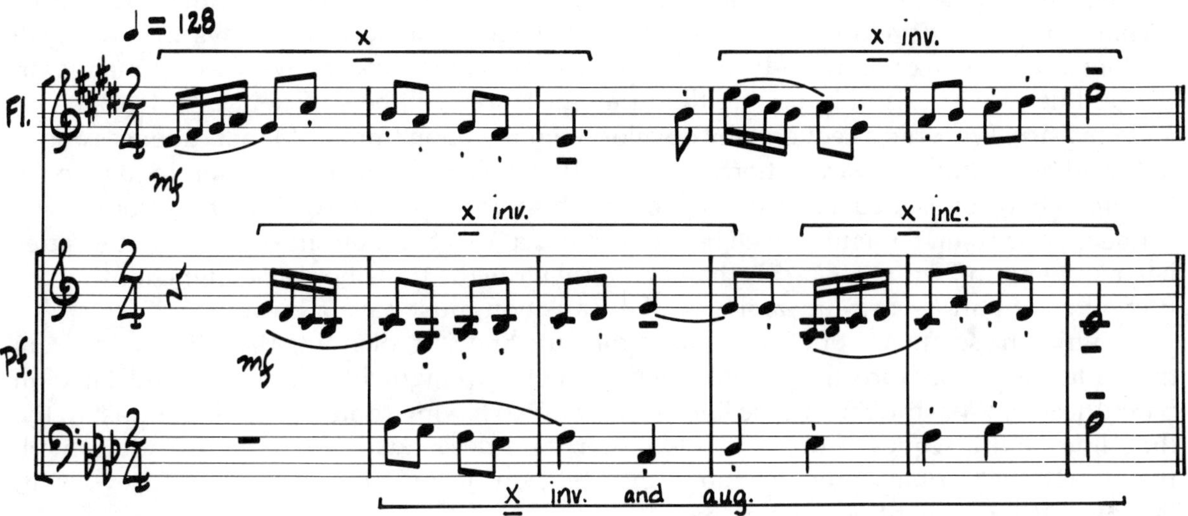

We now proceed to develop this material so that a three-part (*abc*) invention is produced according to our preliminary thoughts.

Example 7.3 *Composing a polytonal invention in ternary (*abc*) form.*

First step: Having already determined the instrumentation, the motives, and certain aspects of the form, we should now make a diagram of the projected work. We need to show the deployment of keys in the three parts, the transitions, and so forth.

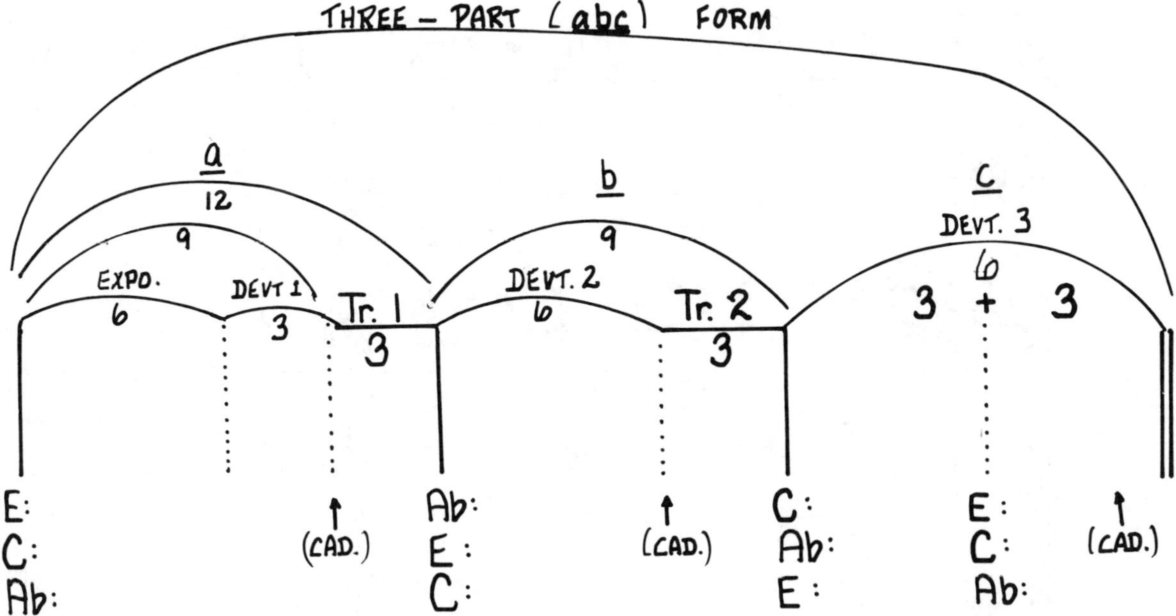

The diagram shows also the location of the cadences and the relative proportions of the three parts. The "exposition" corresponds with the six measures already provided. The three sections marked "development" will utilize the exposed materials in ways that we shall explore as we go. In order to end with the same arrangement of keys, we switch tonalities in the middle of part *c*, and hope that the three measures will be sufficient.

Second step: We write a sequentially developmental section (mm. 7–9) that cadences and is followed by a modulatory transition (mm. 10–12). It might be well, in the latter, to reduce the texture to two voices, or at least to thin it out with short rests in one or two of the voices. The connection with m. 6 might as well be worked out at this time; our next group of measures begins, therefore, with m. 6 rather than m. 7. We write the transition *only* after choosing the first notes of part *b*—to be meaningful, the transition must have a destination.

We write the sequences of *x* fragments in the flute line first, planning them backward from the cadence, to be sure they would end properly. (Fragments, here, are indicated in parentheses.) We write the middle line with a view to having some rhythmic contrast to the flute line, and a sequence that ascends rather than descends. Lastly, the bass line, with further contrast, which provides more an extension of mm. 1–6 than motion beyond it, because of the similarity of mm. 6 and 10.

The first beat of m. 10 elides the cadence and the transition, in which a series of suspensions (or tied anticipations) make use of the *x* motive in augmentation (this appeared previously only in the bass line), while the bass line thins out and assists the (three) modulations. Chromatic notes are introduced in the upper lines to prepare us for the keys of the next part, *b*, which thus are already established by the time we reach m. 13.

Third step: We sketch part *b.* Initially, we draw the bar lines, of course, and the signatures for mm. 13 and 22. We decide to use triple counterpoint here, putting the bass line of part *a* in the flute line; the right-hand line of mm. 1–6 is assigned to the left hand, and the flute line is now played by the right hand. For a bit of contrast, we have the lines—which began originally on their respective tonics—begin on their dominants. This requires a minor adjustment in the right-hand line, m. 13. The flute line is able to explore new (higher) tessitura. To provide a tonic rather than a dominant cadence in m. 18, the *x* motive is varied in the bass line. Since that measure (18) elides cadence and transition, the latter is really four measures long—one measure longer than indicated on the diagram, and longer than the transition at the end of part *a,* with which it otherwise bears a very close resemblance. In the transition we plan *back* from m. 22, to ensure good voice leading (stepwise motion, here, in all voices). The texture is again a bit thinner; the syncopated line formerly in the flute is now in the bass line; the legato quarter-notes falling stepwise resemble those in mm. 10–12.

Fourth step: To ensure fulfillment of our planned form, we first put in our key signatures at the proper places. Part *c* is short, only six measures—we hope it will not seem excessively so. To be sure the work ends properly, we must see to it that the energies are consumed, as it were. A ritenuto, similar to reining in a race horse, will undoubtedly help. We must work out adroitly the connections between the third and fourth measures of part *c* so they seem natural and unforced. There is no transition between these two halves of part *c,* and we may wish to make this clear by having 2+2+2 in at least one voice as a structural counterpoint to a 3+3 in one of the others. The augmented *a* probably should not be used again—it is too long and too leisurely. Stretto is our best means of securing the sense of compactness and tension that will, in retrospect, be the justification for the brevity of this part in contrast to parts *a* and *b.*

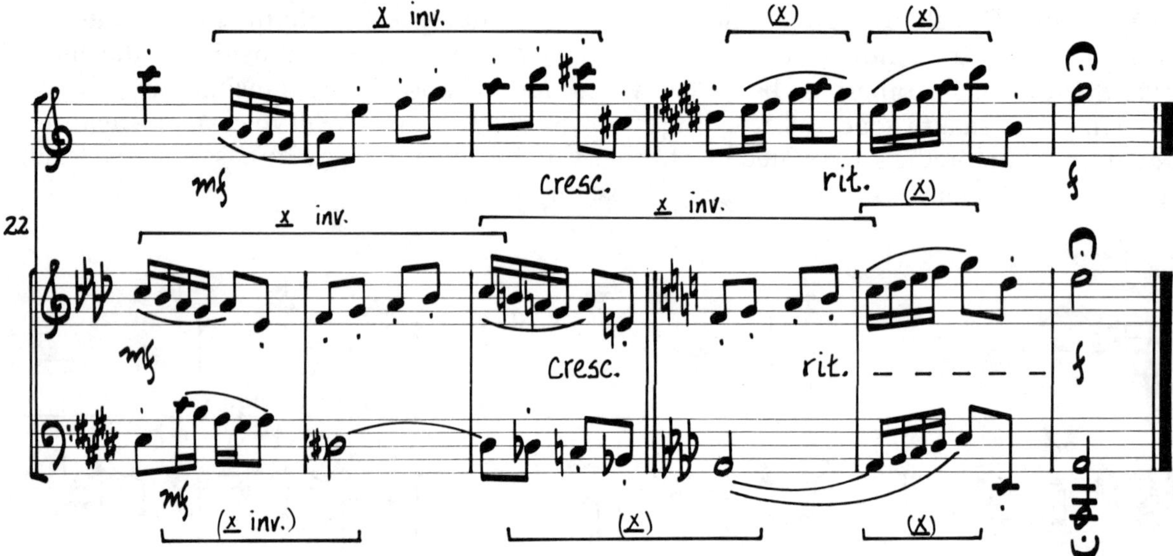

After the work was completed, we realized that the tempo had not been indicated. We determined it and added it to the score. The dynamic level seemed to rest a bit too much on a plateau. The reduced tensions of the transitions suggested *piano* rather than *mezzo forte,* and the return to *mezzo forte* could now be used to reinforce the motive entries at the beginnings of parts *b* and *c.* At the very end, for similar strengthening of the ritenuto that precedes the cadence, a crescendo to *forte* seemed an appropriate addition.

Readers should describe in their own words, each of the three examples we have set forth. A critical evaluation would be useful, with some thoughts regarding possible alternatives for improvement, where that seems desirable, or for equally viable solutions to the same general technical problems.

Exercise 7.1 *Make several precompositional plans for a variety of three-part compositions, using the examples of this chapter as models. Each plan should include a diagram and an accompanying brief essay. The compositions should approach ternary form in a variety of ways and be for different performance media.*

Exercise 7.2 *Following approval of one or more of the plans, commence work on the* a *part and provide comments on your intentions, the problems as you see them, and your proposed solutions.*

Exercise 7.3 *Following completion of the preceding exercises, work similarly on the other parts. Make revisions as needed, and explain the reasons for the alterations. Following completion of the work and a performance, write an objective critique of your music, noting both merits and problems requiring further attention.*

8. Composing a Compound Binary or Ternary Form

If the designs of small binary and small ternary forms are understood, it is a small step to the large or compound binary and ternary forms. Compound form, in this instance, is understood as *ABA,* itself a ternary form, in which each of the three parts is either a small binary or a small ternary form, and in which A^2 is a restatement of A^1 without the inner repetitions. The basic types are as follows.[1]

(a) Both *A* and *B* are two-part forms.

```
┌─A¹─┐   ┌──B──┐  ┌─A²─┐
‖: a : ‖: b : ‖: c : ‖: d : ‖ a | b ‖
```

(b) *A* is three-part, *B* is two-part.

```
┌───A¹────┐   ┌──B──┐   ┌──A²──┐
‖: a¹ : ‖: b a² : ‖ : c : ‖: d : ‖ a¹ | b a² ‖
```

(c) Both *A* and *B* are three-part.

```
┌───A¹────┐   ┌───B────┐   ┌──A²──┐
‖ : a¹ : ‖ : b a² : ‖ : c¹ : ‖: d c² : ‖ a¹ | b a² ‖
```

In stylized dances of the Baroque and Classic eras, repetition of A^2 is usually of the da capo type—A^1 is performed a second time, A^2 is not written out. As indicated above, the inner repetitions are omitted.

Part three (A^2) is written out in a menuetto- or scherzo-type movement only where

1. See *KMF,* Chapter 14.

necessary (if there are minor variants or if the repetitions normally *not* made are, in fact, to be observed). In slow movements, A^2 is always written out.[2]

As a rule, each of the large parts (*A* and *B*) ends with a strong tonic cadence. The small part-forms (*ab* or *aba*) are relatively complete in themselves. Occasionally, however, one finds a retransition leading from *B* to A^2.

There are two types of retransition. In one, *B* dissolves into the retransition without benefit of closing cadence.[3] In the other, there *is* a cadence; the retransition appears postcadentially.[4]

The middle part (*B*) is usually unrelated to *A* in material. The Trio part of the second movement of Mozart's *String Quintet in G minor*, K. 516, is an exception. Here, the Trio (the *B* part) is based upon a motive derived from the postcadential extension at the end of *A*.[5] It is customary for *B* to provide a somewhat contrasting mood (but not tempo), either in the same key and mode, or in the parallel major (if *A* is in minor). Other closely related keys are sometimes used.

Compound forms are most frequently found in the paired dances of the Baroque era (Minuet I-II-I, or Gavotte I-II-I, for example), and in the Minuet- (or Scherzo-) and -Trio movement of the Classic and Romantic sonata, chamber work, and symphony.

Extension of the *ABA* form to *ABABA* (Scherzo-Trio-Scherzo-Trio-Scherzo) is found in Beethoven's symphonies No. Four and No. Seven, and a variant of this idea appears in Brahms's *Symphony No. 2 in D major,* where the second Trio (B^2) is a transformation of the first.

Shostakovich, in the Scherzo movement of his *Symphony No. 1,* uses the themes of both *A* and *B*, simultaneously, toward the end of A^2, an idea similar to that found in a double fugue.

The term *Trio* as a description of the middle part, in this form, derives from the practice in the Baroque era of reducing the instrumentation of such a work, when scored for large ensemble, to three instruments. The term remains, but not the practice—except, perhaps, a tendency to use a lighter texture and (in an orchestral work) to reduce the number of performing instruments and to lower the dynamic level. The term is also used to describe the second half of a march—many of Sousa's marches, for example, are in form a March-and-Trio, the "Trio" being in effect a second march and, curiously, in the *subdominant* key. This form is a binary one (the first part is not repeated), and there is no return to the tonic key.

In our critique of Example 7.2, we considered it possible that the Scherzo would be more effective as part of a Scherzo-and-Trio movement than alone. In the interest of improving the status of the Scherzo, and in view of our space limitations, we shall work out a compatible Trio to serve as midsection (*B*), the Scherzo of Example 7.2 to serve as A^1 and (without the repetitions) also as A^2. We will plan to have *no* retransition between *B* and A^2. Since the Scherzo ends a bit abruptly on the last beat of the measure in a^2, we may decide to add a brief coda.[6] The coda in one sense extends A^2, but in another sense it is an extension of the whole *ABA* design. The distinction is evident if one compares the following diagrams.

2. See Mozart's *Piano Sonata in D major,* K. 576, and *KMF,* page 126. Not only is part three written out, but in none of the parts are there repetitions of the subdivisions. Thus, *ABA* = *aba+cdc+aba.* There are retransitions at the ends of *d* and *B,* and a coda following the second *A.*
3. See *KMF,* Example 13.6.
4. See *KMF,* examples 13.7 and 14.3.
5. See *KMF,* Example 14.4.
6. For precedent, see Beethoven's symphonies Nos. 3, 4, 7 and 9, and *Piano Sonata,* Op. 2, no. 3.

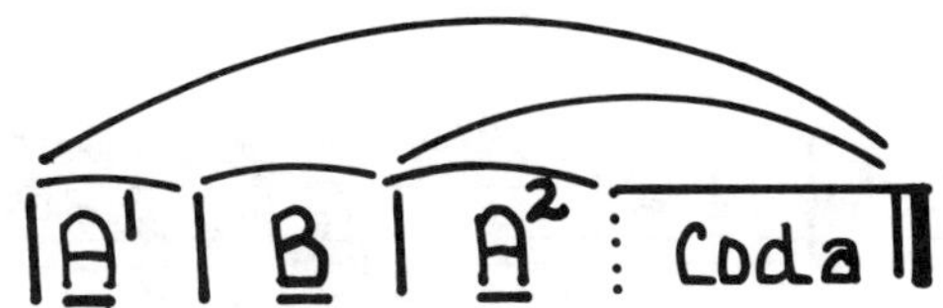

Mozart, in his *Symphony No. 40 in G minor,* the third movement, has a codetta *within* the Menuetto (end of a^2), and of course it should be performed at the end of each *A* part. The conductor Frederick Stock, for many years music director of the Chicago Symphony, perhaps thinking that Mozart had not indicated his intentions clearly, used to omit this codetta before repeating ba^2—he evidently regarded the codetta as an extension of the *aba* form as a whole, not (as Mozart wrote it) as an extension of a^2. An interesting case of an analytical mind at work but—I think—on the wrong track.

Example 8.1 *Composing a Trio for the Scherzo of Example 7.2 (making a Compound Ternary Form).*

Our projected Trio should be more relaxed than the Scherzo. It will be the same length but, for contrast, the first part (c^1) will be longer rather than shorter than part three (c^2). We use the same combination of keys (C and E) and small ternary form, but employ the letters *cdc* for the Trio to distinguish the materials from *aba* of the Scherzo. A brief coda will follow the second Scherzo (A^2), using materials drawn from the Trio, to suggest in a teasing way the return of the Trio, as Beethoven does in his Seventh and Ninth symphonies.

Motivic material of the Scherzo consisted largely of leaps suggesting chord outlines. For contrast, the Trio will use mostly stepwise motion. To relate the Trio to the Scherzo, we borrow the running eighths of mm. 8–9 in the Scherzo, plus the quarter-note figure of m. 10 ( ). These ideas may be used together in counterpoint, in sequence, and in imitation, and of course varied in any number of ways. We decide on the measure lengths (6+6+4) and, with the bar lines drawn, get to work on c^1. A diagram of the entire compound-form before us is a distinct help in making plans.

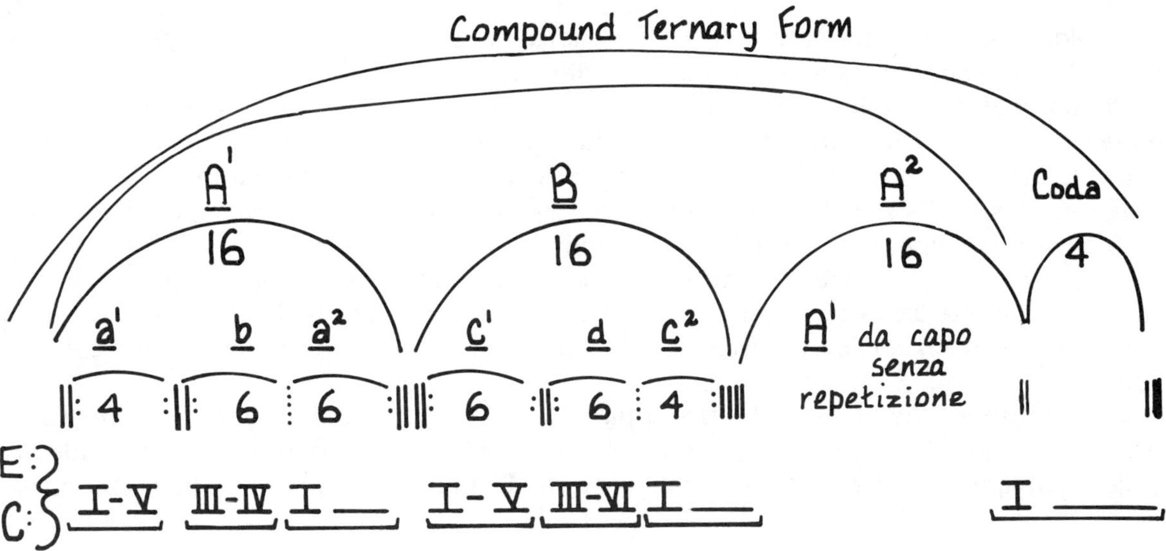

Thinking that it would help narrow the choice of suitable tones and at the same time provide a sense of direction, we decide on a harmonic scheme that will operate simultaneously in C major (left-hand part) and E major (right-hand part). As in the Scherzo, the violin participates in the chords of both keys. Starting with our basic framework (tonic to begin with, dominant at the end of c^1), we proceed down a series of thirds and then move to the cadence, thus: I VI IV II V-II V. There is one chord per measure except for m. 5, which has two (V-II), with the supertonic serving as an auxiliary to the dominant.

We begin our writing with the running eighths, starting in the bass on the tonic; above it, we write the quarter-note figure in contrary motion, while the violin provides pizzicato double-stops in harmonic support: C-E is in C:I, B-E in E:I, E is the common tone, C-B-A a good line.

M. 2 continues the ideas in the piano part, using double counterpoint. The upper line begins on C, as did the lower line in m. 1, but the C is a C♯; we use four sharps to provide the scale of E major. Since C♯ is the sixth scale degree in E, and VI is the chord we have chosen for

m. 2, C♯ nicely serves several purposes. The violin part is related chiefly to the tonality of the bass line, but E as common tone relates C:VI (A-C-E) to E:VI (C♯-E-G♯).

We decide, in m. 3, that the violin should set forth the motive of running eighths. It begins on the fifth of the predetermined chord, not on the root as in mm. 1 and 2. The right hand repeats the left-hand part of m. 2, except that it is in E, not in C. The left hand provides the root and third of C:IV, discreetly avoiding the fifth (C), which would clash with C♯ above.

The two-beat rest in the violin line serves two purposes: to allow the performer time to readjust the bow arm to play arco instead of pizzicato, and to permit a delayed entry, providing surprise appropriate for this genre.

In m. 4, the left-hand part thickens to two basically parallel lines. The right hand plays triads (three notes) instead of intervals (two notes). Violin and left-hand part are in tonal accord (C:II); the A is a common tone linking C:II and E:II.

Mm. 5–6 emphasize the V-chord. Accents (*sf*) are applied to both II and V. For the cadence, we return the violin to pizzicato, which thus serves as an enveloping frame for the arco line in mm. 3–5. To secure a strong cadence, we allow the left hand simply to support the harmony. Running eighths ascend two octaves in the right-hand line. The quarter-rest provides surprise. On the first beat of m. 6, B serves as common tone in C:V (G-B-D) and E:V (B-D♯-F♯). A quadruple-stop in the violin takes advantage of the open strings G and D. A♯, in the right-hand line, is intended to suggest the dominant key (B major). Our final notes, at the end of m. 6, lead nicely into the repetition of c^1.

Turning now to the middle section, *d*, we plan the harmonic framework: III IV V VI—, with one chord per measure for three measures, followed by VI extended for three measures. This provides contrast to the design of c^1, and the prolonged VI will be identified with the retransition. It will be recalled that extended harmonies characteristically are associated either with tonic (extended *repose*) or non-tonic (extended *tension*) functions.

For motivic contrast, we abandon the running eighths, but continue to use the other ideas already seen in c^1. We will try to use the quarter-note motive in inversion and stretto, in parallel thirds, contrary motion, and so forth. The violin will play arco only, and vary the motive by using the principle of the displaced octave.

The texture of the retransition should be thinner, the ideas anticipatory of the return of *c*, and leading to it by stepwise motion—which means working back from the end.

Looking at our six measures in retrospect, we see that the texture did not thin out. The drive toward development involved all the voices, and in this respect the result departed from our preconception. It seems to work, all the same.

In m. 7, the outer voices have the quarter-note motive in contrary motion, the violin using octave displacement and a slight change of rhythm on the fourth beat to allow the A to be slurred to the low G♯. In the right hand, E:III is outlined; the other parts relate to C:III.

M. 8 is a varied sequence of m. 7, with violin and right hand exchanging material. In m. 9, rests create fragmentation of another sequence; the violin entry a beat late, at the climax, creates the effect of stretto with the bass line.

M. 10 is the high point in the crescendo, but the nadir of the violin line, which is a modified inversion of its m. 7. The two keyboard lines have a stretto of the motive in contrary motion, with the lines doubled in thirds. The next two measures prolong both the harmony, as planned, and the use of parallel thirds in the right-hand part. We observe here also the motive in augmentation, E-G♯ serving as the *end* of the motive in quarter-notes (mm. 10) and as the *beginning* of the motive augmented to half-notes (mm. 10–12).[7]

At the end of the retransition (m. 12), the violin trails off to nothing, but the last note (E) anticipates the first notes in m. 13. The quarter-note motive in the right-hand part similarly prepares us for its use in the next measure. The left-hand line prolongs A minor (C:VI); the fifth-beat eighth-notes are consistent with C:VI and lead directly to the note C in m. 13. The last quarter-notes, right hand, m. 12, anticipate the first notes of c^2.

Now to the composing of part three (c^2). We want to limit it to four measures, which means considerable concentration. Its end must lead equally well to the repeat of dc^2 and to the repeat of the Scherzo (A^2). Since it begins and ends on I, the middle measures must be chosen: we decide on VI and IV, to provide a plagal cadence.

In c^2 (mm. 13–16), we begin with the violin part, again using pizzicato, but (in variation) triads instead of intervals, using common tones and a minimum of linear motion in mm. 13–14. The ascending eighths, arco, reappear, but on the first beat, not the third, using C:IV for beats 1–2, E:IV for beats 3–5, with stepwise motion to m. 16, where I appears in both C and E.

7. Brahms often uses this device in retransitions. See *KMF*, page 282, for an example.

In the piano parts, m. 13 restates m. 1; m. 14 is but slightly varied, the triad on beat 5 imitating the violin chord sound. Looking at the right-hand line in mm. 15–16, we find a departure from c^1: the eighth-note motive is used in simultaneous contrary motion against the violin, resulting in a rare instance of parallel octaves (over the bar line). M. 16 corresponds to m. 6, now E:I instead of E:V (or B:I). The left-hand line, in mm. 15–16, restates the (rhythmically displaced) quarter-note figure, so as to provide the desired sense of IV-to-I, clearly rather different from the end of c^1.

The dynamic scheme for c^2 differs from c^1, as well. Although similar in rising from *p* to *f*, it does so with a single crescendo rather than in two waves. There are no problems of connection with respect to the return to c^1 or to the beginning of the Scherzo (A^1).

Our remaining task is to devise the coda. We shall endeavor to do this in four measures, as per our diagram, and limit ourselves to tonic harmony throughout, that is, C:I and E:I. We will borrow materials from the Trio (*B*). In performance, the coda follows the completion of A^2. There should be indication to this effect in the final version of the score. Classic procedure is to write at the end of the Trio: *Scherzo da capo senza repetizione, poi il Coda* (The Scherzo from the beginning without repetitions, then the Coda).

Except for the final beat, *sfz,* the coda is *p* throughout. Texture is thinned by the full-measure rests in the violin and right-hand parts. The first measure begins somewhat like the Trio (c^1). In m. 2, the violin and left-hand parts repeat m. 1 in double counterpoint: we transpose the violin part from C:I to E:I, of course, and the quarter-note motive from E to C major. M. 3 continues this idea in the two upper lines, while the bass sustains the tonic of C; the scale line in the right hand begins on G♯ instead of E, to provide further sequence rather than repetition of m. 2.

A *sustained* E in the closing measures of the violin part echoes the similar procedure in the right hand of the piano, m. 1 of the coda. The *reinforced* E at the very end is designed to reconcile the two keys: it is the only note that is part of the tonic chord in both C:I and E:I.

Our tonic pedal point, explicit or implied, provides stability throughout. Continuing development of ideas enlists the interest of the listener. The final sforzando is a reminiscence of the close of the Scherzo (A^2).

Exercise 8.1 *Using the Scherzo of Example 7.2 as parts* A^1 *and* A^2 *of a compound ternary form, compose a Trio with materials and structural details different from the one displayed in Example 8.1. Prepare a diagram, a descriptive narrative, and a critique of the completed work.*

Exercise 8.2 *Using only the diagram of the compound ternary form on page 110, compose appropriate music that employs a style and materials different from those used for chapters 7 and 8. Provide a running commentary on your work. Explain minor departures from the preconceived plan. Write a critical appraisal of the completed composition.*

Exercise 8.3 *Make a detailed preliminary diagram of a proposed compound ternary form that is either one of the first two types outlined on page 107 (where* A *and* B *are both two-part forms, or where* A *is three-part and* B *two-part). Plan a dissolution at the end of* B*; a second ending will be needed for that. A retransition then will lead from* B *to* A^2.

Exercise 8.4 *Write a slow movement in compound ternary form, using* aba+cdc+aba *as overall structural outline. There are no inner repeats, and* A^2 *should be a slightly modified repetition of* A^1. *Make a diagram, first; narrative commentary should accompany each stage of your composition; following completion and performance of the work, write an objective evaluation.*

9. Continuity and Discontinuity: Extension, Transition and Retransition, Connection or Separation, Overlap and Elision; Expectation and Surprise

The subtitle of this chapter may appear long and the topics excessive in number. But these topics are closely related concepts pertaining to an aspect of composition that is especially significant in large structures, namely *the expressive and formal functions of various types of continuity and discontinuity.*

A large composition may have a form that is little more than an assembly of small pieces placed end to end, a procedure that is most evident in many relatively primitive Baroque keyboard variations, and in some classical ballets, where set dances (solos, pas de deux, etc.) are short and appear in arbitrary sequence. A song cycle may be unified by a literary idea, though the individual songs are complete in themselves, as in Schubert's *Die Winterreise.* Pre-Wagnerian "number opera," with its alternating and separated recitatives and arias, is held together by its libretto rather than by melodic line or curve.

It is instructive to study Wagner's masterful use of connective tissue, in his later operas particularly. In his Overture to *Die Meistersinger*, several contrasting themes used later in the opera are connected by developmental episodes that are remarkable for their substance and workmanship. Tchaikovsky, more comfortable with the shorter forms required by ballet than with the large design of the symphony, tends in his transitions to rely excessively upon formulas of repetition and sequence, as in the first movement of his *Symphony No. 6* ("Pathetique"); and in *Romeo and Juliet*, the section in the allegro preceding the second theme. Chopin, essentially a miniaturist, wisely avoided larger forms, except in his two early piano concertos, the cello sonata, and the two piano sonatas.

Extension

Extension denotes the expansion of a musical form at the beginning, middle, or end, through means that are partly harmonic and tonal, partly thematic and developmental, sometimes with a tempo change.[1] For an extension to be recognized as such by the listener, it must be heard as something of an appendage. Clearly, this requires the existence of other musical material that is heard as fundamental and complete in itself. If the composer wishes the appendage to be accepted as necessary rather than gratuitous, then it must fulfill a formal and expressive function.

A *preliminary extension* in a large form may appear as a slow introduction, for instance to a fast movement in sonata or sonata-rondo form.[2] It may contain material that: 1) is not used again (Tchaikovsky, *Piano Concerto in B♭ minor*, first movement); 2) is used again but only in the coda (Schubert, *Symphony in C major*, "the Great," first movement); 3) is used in both the development section and the coda (Beethoven, *Piano Sonata in C minor*, Op. 13, first movement)[3]; or 4) contains the thematic cells of one or more movements that follow it (Beethoven, *Leonore Overtures No. 2* and *No. 3*, and the Bartók *String Quartet No. 6*). Prolonged preliminary extension is usually multi-sectional and may involve considerable modulation (as if the composer were probing for the right key), but these tonal shifts are usually details in what proves to be an expanded V-chord, or motion that leads to this chord, providing a large formal anacrusis.

Brief preliminary extensions (introductions) have been observed in earlier chapters—see the opening four measures of the *Agnus Dei,* Example 6.1, and the first six measures of the song, Example 7.1. The function in each instance was to prepare the listener for the mood, character, and style; to introduce some of the motives; and (a practical concern) to prepare the singer for his initial vocal entry. (More extended introductions appear in *KMF,* examples 20.3, 23.3, 25.6, 25.7, and 25.9–12, and tables 23.1 and 23.5.)

Opera overtures or preludes serve similar functions for the acts that follow, sometimes foreshadowing later materials, and either lead directly to the scene that follows (as in Mozart's *Don Giovanni*) or end with a pause before the curtain goes up (as in Beethoven's *Fidelio*). Perhaps the largest introduction ever written is Wagner's entire opera, *Das Rheingold,* intended as a prelude to the three-opera cycle *Das Ring des Nibelungen.*

Introductions may be composed after the main structure has been sketched or (better still) completed, because the things to be done are more clearly understood at that time. There is considerable evidence that most composers have recognized this fact.[4]

1. See *KMF,* Chapter 6 (extensions of the phrase), Chapter 8 (extensions of the period), page 116 (extension in small song forms), page 249 (extended rondo forms), and the listings in the index on page 336.
2. See symphonic first movements by Beethoven (Nos. 1, 2, 4, and 7) and Brahms (No. 1); and last movements in Beethoven's Nos. 1, 3, and 9, Brahms's No. 1. For twentieth-century examples, the first movements of Bartók's *Concerto for Orchestra* and the *Sonata for Two Pianos and Percussion;* his *String Quartet No. 6* has thematically related introductions prior to each movement except the last, and *that* is an expansion of the ideas in the introductions.
3. See *KMF,* Example 2.4.
4. Mozart is thought to have composed his overture to *The Marriage of Figaro* a few hours before the premiere performance. Following the completion of his opera *Fidelio,* Beethoven continued to write overtures until they numbered four in all. Wagner could hardly have written his *Meistersinger* overture

The composition example and exercise that should follow at this point can hardly be written without a larger structure having already been written. We therefore defer until a later chapter the methodology to pursue in our usual step-by-step approach.

Extensions during the course of a work are very common and of course vary in size and function. For the most part, they create additional interest and intensity. They often have a denser and more polyphonic texture if the main structure is primarily homophonic. If the extension is in a repeated part—such as the recapitulation in sonata form, or in a second or third *A*-section in rondo form—one hears it as an *interpolation,* a supplement to the expected restatement.[5] The determination of need for such extensions is impossible without the existence of an already partly sketched work. That, and the means to be used in their realization, must once again be postponed until a later chapter, when we shall be considering larger forms.

Extensions at the end are commonly described as codas or codettas.[6] Since these sections usually follow cadences, it is well to remember the distinction between *pre*cadential and *post*cadential extensions.[7] A long terminal extension characteristically appears only at the end of a large work. When it appears at the end of the *last* movement of a multi-movement composition, it assumes the role of coda to the *entire* work. The codas that close Beethoven's symphonies No. 3 and No. 5 would be absurdly long if one were to consider them as terminating only their last movements.

Occasionally, final extensions include references to one or more previous movements, as in Dvořák's *Symphony in E minor* ("From the New World") and Brahms's *Symphony No. 3 in F major.* Multi-movement works prevailingly in somber minor mode may use the coda as a final effort to wear an optimistic face and end brightly in major (see Mozart's *Concerto in D minor for Piano and Orchestra,* K. 466).[8]

Transition and retransition

Transitions and retransitions, like extension, are auxiliary musical structures. They differ from extension, however, in that their function is not to enlarge and expand a design, but to create a kind of aural corridor or passageway from one structural detail to another. A transition leads us from one more-or-less complete element in the design to another, whereas a retransition does an about-face and leads us from a secondary structural unit to a restatement of a previously heard unit. Thus, in an *ABA* design, there could be a transition between parts one and two, a retransition between *B* and the second *A.*[9]

---

without advance knowledge of the musical substance of the opera as a whole. On the other hand, some introductions would appear necessarily to have been composed *during or before* the main structure, because they contain the seeds of further development, as in the Beethoven *Piano Sonata in C minor,* Op. 13, first movement, already mentioned.

5. For examples, see *KMF,* Example 21.6, where a cadenza extends the second *B* in an *ABACABA* rondo; Example 22.1, where the five-part rondo is expanded to *ABACBA;* Example 22.2, in which the middle *A* of an *ABABA* form is expanded by an interpolated fugato; and Example 24.4, a sonatina form in which a development section is interpolated in the course of the recapitulation.

6. See *KMF,* page 135, footnote 3.

7. See *KMF,* page 76.

8. See *KMF,* Example 24.7.

9. See *KMF,* index, under "transition" and "retransition."

We observed these concepts functioning in small forms in Chapter 7 (see pages 76, 78–79, 81–82, 84, and footnote 5 on page 70) and Chapter 8 (Example 8.1, mm. 11–12, pages 89–90), where we had the opportunity to compare the relatively static extensions with the transitions and retransitions, which were dynamic and tension building.

The same qualities tend to be evident in large-scale works, except that the structures tend to be more complex, frequently with a number of structural subdivisions; and they have a direction that is more a wavy than a straight line. The reason for this difference is largely psychological: the simple, straight-line approach is too obvious if sustained beyond a certain point. The composer's task, in this case, is to make clear to the listener that the underlying direction, or motion is a step from "here" to "there," but that instead of moving with a single jump, we have in a more leisurely manner explored some of the tonal scenery in the side roads and byways. The transition between Principal and Second Theme, and the retransition leading to the recapitulation in Brahms's *Symphony No. 2 in D major* are good cases in point.[10]

The transition takes up nearly half (thirty-six measures) of the eighty-one-measure principal-theme group, of which it is the latter part. Ostensibly engaged simply in modulating from D major to F♯ minor, the part has three subdivisions in which the principal theme motives *a* and *b* are developed, lyrically at first, then somewhat dramatically and contrapuntally, and finally playfully, in diminution and sequence.[11]

The retransition appears in mm. 282–301, the last twenty measures of the 219-measure development section, and although it follows tradition in stressing the dominant of the main key, it continues the development process to the very end. Grouped 8+8+4, the twenty measures are devoted initially to the *b* motive (the chord outline), secondly to a mixture of three motives in polyphonic texture, and finally to the neighboring-tone motive, *a*, in augmentation. There is a remarkable dissolution in which development and recapitulation overlap through careful harmonization of the *a* motive—the development technically ends with a II^7 chord, the recapitulation begins on I^6_4, and only after the structural hurdle has been left behind does the six-four resolve to V and then to I.[12]

The recapitulation portion of the second movement of Beethoven's *String Quartet in D major*, Op. 18, no. 3, includes a very extended transition (mm. 59–95) that is longer than the principal theme of which it is an outgrowth (mm. 47–58). Combined, they form the principal-theme group. To appreciate fully what the composer has done here, one should compare the recapitulation with the exposition from which it is a considerable departure.[13]

Unlike the exposition, where the two themes are in B♭ and F, respectively, here they are in the same key (B♭). Therefore, to be effective the transition had to be abbreviated (because no modulation is called for), or extended by means of interpolated modulatory episodes. Beethoven here opted for the latter.

Using principal-theme material for the most part, he develops his ideas in several episodes that modulate from B♭ to D♭ to F minor to B♭ minor (outlining the B♭ minor chord in his choice of keys), at which point there is a half-cadence. The major triad at this point serves as penultimate chord in the return to B♭ major, and as convenient pivot in shifting from B♭ minor to B♭ major. The tonic key now has the freshness of sound needed for the second theme to be effective.

10. See *KMF*, Example 23.4, mm. 44–81 and 282–301.
11. See *KMF*, pages 278–279.
12. See *KMF*, pages 281–282.
13. See *KMF*, Example 24.4.

The opening five and the closing five measures of this transition correspond to parallel measures in the exposition, which suggests that they were either actually written first or that the overall strategy was conceived before the tactical details had been worked out. From this fact alone, one may derive an important lesson in composition.

Connection or separation

It has been suggested in the preceding pages that successive parts of large compositional structures may be placed end to end; they may also be separated by silence, or they may be joined in a sort of formal embrace by the use of elision or overlap.

Connection or separation of parts are made, clearly, by the intention of the composer. Sometimes, it is a matter that is simply determined by style, habit, and custom. The Baroque rondeau has parts that are discrete, with contrasting sections that end in strong cadences; whereas the rondo of the Classic era normally has retransitions leading from the contrasting sections to the several returns of the *A*-part. In the former, there is more separation between parts, in the latter, more continuous flow.

There is similar opportunity for the composer to choose between flow and separation at the point in sonata form where development ends and recapitulation begins. There is considerable flow and continuity in the *Symphony No. 2*, by Brahms, already discussed on page 97. On the other hand, there is a decided break, well indicated by the *Luftpause* (breath pause), the tempo change, and the discontinuity of lines in Stravinsky's *Sonata for Two Pianos*, first movement, mm. 52–53.[14]

Overlap and elision

Overlap and elision are procedures designed to assist in providing continuity. The Brahms illustration just mentioned is an example of overlap, created largely by the harmonic plan, which is so designed that the resolution to tonic harmony occurs well beyond the structural joint. Another illustration, in a shorter work, is m. 11 in *Fugue No. 2 in C minor* of *The Well-Tempered Clavier*, Volume 1, by Bach, in which the first half may be interpreted by the ear as a sequential continuation of the preceding two-measure episode, but also as the beginning of the next statement of the subject, a deliberate and calculated use of ambiguity.[15]

Elision is a related but slightly different concept.[16] A single beat, sometimes just one note, serves at the same time as termination of what has preceded it and as beginning of what follows. In the same Bach fugue, m. 29, beat 3, the note C is both cadence termination (ending the previous phrase) and *beginning* of the tonic pedal point that underlies the final subject statement.

Elision should not be confused with a common procedure found in Classic and Romantic sonata and rondo forms, in which a retransition dissolves in such a manner as to lead to a restatement (of the main theme) that begins with the tonic chord. This tonic serves as resolution of the dominant chord that characteristically precedes it, but it is *not* the

14. See *KMF*, Example 23.5.
15. See *KMF*, Example 19.10.
16. See *KMF*, index, page 336.

termination of the previous structural division—there is, in other words, no cadence here. A useful comparison may be made in a single work, Beethoven's *Piano Sonata in C minor,* Op. 13, second movement.[17] M. 51 marks the beginning of part A^3, m. 50 the end of part C, the closing measures of which constitute the retransition. The tonic harmony in m. 51 serves but one function, as the beginning of A^3. But in m. 66, the tonic chord serves both as cadential termination of the part (A^3), which is a period in form, and as the beginning of the coda.

The difference between overlap and elision is clearly seen in canonic works, where *phrases* overlap, creating a texture of continuity for the duration of the canon.[18]

A rare instance in which a musical section of substantial length illustrates both elision and overlap is present in Beethoven's *Leonore Overture No. 3.* The overture as a whole is in sonata form with slow introduction and coda. The exposition section modulates from the principal tonal area, C major, to E major. The recapitulation is highly irregular, in that the first part has been altered in a manner to make necessary a double interpretation.

We are on solid ground when we hear the *fortissimo* second statement of the first theme in the full orchestra, at m. 378, but the preceding section (mm. 330–377) does not correspond to the first statement of the main theme in the exposition (mm. 37–68). It does replace it, and it has certain thematic and harmonic and textural features in common with it, and it, too, closes with an extended V^7 over a tonic pedal point. But it is not primarily in the tonic key, and is rather an emphasis upon the dominant (G) normally associated with the retransition portion of the development section.

This section is an *elision* in that *something has been omitted* (the first statement in its original substance and key), and it creates *overlap* because in one sense it is part of the development section and in another sense it *is* the (substitute) first statement of the first theme in the recapitulation. The diagram below shows how one might represent this ambiguity in graphic form. One can only speculate on the reasons for Beethoven's having composed this in the manner indicated—possibly it involved his determination to avoid an excess of tonic key in the recapitulation, always a problem when both themes are in the tonic, particularly in view of the anticipated use of the tonic in an extensive coda.

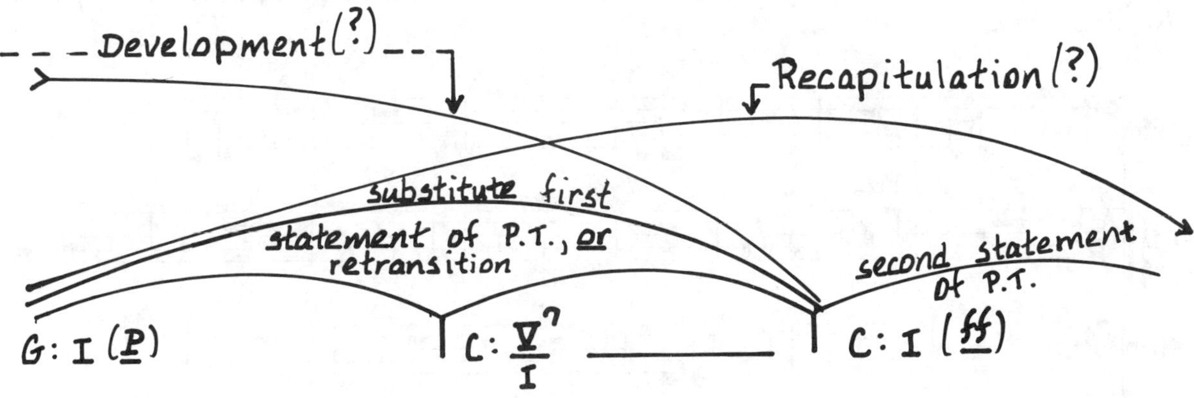

17. See *KMF,* Example 21.5.
18. See *KMF,* Exercise 1 in Chapter 17. Compare this illustration with Example 16.4 in the same text (*Variations on a Theme by Joseph Haydn*, by Brahms), in which measure one of a five-measure ground bass serves quite frequently as both the beginning of one phrase and the end of the preceding one.

Expectation and surprise

Expectation and surprise, like beauty and ugliness, reside more in the mind of the observer than in the object observed. Nevertheless, artists who know their craft and their audience, can make subtle use of these elements for expressive purposes.

Expectation appears most commonly in such techniques as repetition, sequence, the circle of harmonic fifths, and so forth. Even surprise, which one would perhaps not expect to be codified, has its favorite devices—the evaded and the deceptive cadence. The latter became so common in Wagner (considerably outnumbering the realized cadences) that they became the new expectations!

It is not uncommon, in hearing some work for the first time, to say at some point or another that the music sounds as though it were going to be a theme and variations (because of the simple and symmetrical design of an opening theme) or a fugue (because of the unaccompanied melodic line and the terse and aphoristic character of the line itself). There is a measure of satisfaction to be gained in having such expectations fulfilled.[19] Sometimes, of course, one anticipates that the music will simply go through the motions of following a time-worn prescription, and in that case there is more ennui than joy in hearing the prophecy fulfilled. Beginning composers, eager to display their talents, must learn to use them with conviction and necessity, and try to avoid the pitfall of rediscovery of the wheel.

An excess of zeal may lead one to create so many surprises that seem unjustifiable in context, that they cancel each other out by causing the listener to expect them. As with the judicious choice of condiments in gastronomy, the effectiveness of surprise is in inverse proportion to its frequency. Well-known uses of surprise include Haydn's *"Surprise" Symphony;* the opening chord in Beethoven's *Symphony No. 1* (V^7 of IV, rather daring in its day); the premature entry of the horns in sounding the recapitulation of the first theme in Beethoven's *Symphony No. 3* (the "Eroica"); and the use of alla breve (₵) for four measures in the latter part of the ¾-metered scherzo of the same symphony. A "false recapitulation" in the development section may heighten the expectation of a true one.[20] There is a capricious one-measure delay in the timpani part in the scherzo movement of Beethoven's *Symphony No. 9.*

19. See Leonard B. Meyer, *Emotion and Meaning in Music,* University of Chicago Press, 1956, Chapter 2.
20. See, for example, Brahms's *Sonata in G major for Violin and Piano,* Op. 78, first movement, mm. 140–141 and 148–149. The recapitulation proper begins at m. 156.

Brahms, in the fourth movement of his *Sonata in D minor for Violin and Piano*, has (in the exposition section) a transition that suggests a modulation to the dominant key, A minor, because of the extended use of a:V; but this harmony (an E-major triad) deceptively resolves to a:VI, an F-major triad that surprisingly turns out to be F:I—an ingenious new use of an old device (the dominant pedal point).

Expectation is an element that is inherent in the use of motives. Schoenberg's *String Quartet No. 4* employs the rhythmic idea 𝅗𝅥𝅗𝅥|♫♫♩♩ as an important thematic and structural element, sometimes with the original melodic contour with which it is associated in mm. 1–2, sometimes not. Part of the pleasure in hearing a fugue comes from the recognition of the fugue subject, which one expects to recur with some frequency. Listeners familiar with the music of the Classic and early Romantic periods have certain expectations respecting the sonata form, rondo, variations, and so forth. Since no two works are ever exactly alike, listeners are never quite sure exactly how and when their expectations may be fulfilled, and are prepared to be surprised.

Only the composers themselves know when they have found the balance between the opposing needs of expectation and surprise. There is no recipe or formula for "correct" balance, and no substitute for eternal vigilance in the objective evaluation of one's own work. Step number one is to be *aware*.

No composition exercises appear in this chapter for reasons already indicated. Analysis of larger works by significant composers of all periods, with special attention given to the way the ideas we have discussed have been realized, should be of incalculable assistance to readers when they embark on their own personal voyages of discovery.

10. Developmental Procedures: Repetition and Contrast

The development of musical ideas essentially involves the use of *variation*. It may be recalled that in the arts generally, and in music particularly, successions of events demonstrate the principles of *repetition* (which creates unity), *contrast* (which provides diversity), or a combination of the two: variation. If a given musical idea combines pitch sequences, rhythmic ideas, harmonic design, instrumental color, dynamic levels, texture, and so forth, and this given idea is repeated with one or several of the elements altered, then we have variation. Development without variation (that is, development without repetition or without contrast) is clearly not possible.

It is our purpose in this chapter to concentrate on the idea of development, first as observed in earlier chapters of this book, then as observed in the literature, and finally to provide some exercises to develop skill in this particular aspect of composition.

In Example 2.1, five motives provided structural unity; *variation in their use* through dynamic change, retrograde motion, elision, fragmentation, and so on, was the basis of "development," along with brief passages that had no references to these motives.

Example 2.3 deliberately used *variation form* as a means of development, the details of which are elaborated on page 21. The unfolding of ideas in Example 3.1 may be observed in the development of the motive (see Table 3.1) in four sections, as outlined on page 24, the first of which included a pedal point, the second a chromatic bass line, the third a plan for root motion, and the fourth a postcadential extension.

Imitation of the motive, in a polyphonic texture, is a characteristic of the development in Example 4.1. There is no motive to provide unity in Example 4.2; here the emphasis is more on the contrast between the lines, with the demands of logical continuity taken care of more within each of the lines than by agreement among them. Distinctive use of rhythmic-retrograde and section-retrograde motion provides some degree of "development."

Example 5.1 develops a one-measure motive in prevailingly homophonic texture, using varied harmonies, changing dynamics, and brief introduction of polyphonic texture for more contrast.

The choral work in Example 6.1 is unified by its text. The homophonic texture in which the motives are first exposed yields in time to a polyphonic texture, with imitation. A brief instrumental prelude, interlude, and codetta provide color (timbre) contrast, at the same time using motives that are derived largely from the choral part.

In Example 6.2, we find imitation, sometimes in inversion, with a carefully prepared bass line the phrases of which emphasize the all-important tonic and dominant notes at beginnings and endings. Occasional pizzicato instead of arco provides additional contrast, particularly needed at the crucial climactic point.

Example 6.3, in part one, uses sequence, imitation, double counterpoint, and, for contrast, occasional parallel motion; in part two, changed texture, dynamics and tessitura for contrast, as well as augmentation and double augmentation. Careful treatment of tessitura makes possible a suggestion of an additional voice in the polyphonic texture. Overlapping groups help provide continuity; a pause for breath (indicated by comma), momentary discontinuity. As a final polyphonic fillip, triple augmentation is employed, with fragmentation of the motive above it.

Review of chapters 7 and 8 will yield similar dividends. The topics discussed in Chapter 9 may be observed to be concerned also with the general idea of development.

The literature respecting procedures of development is inexhaustible. Space limitations limit our consideration to four compositions, of which certain parts are illustrated in *KMF*. It is hoped that the reader will have access to the full scores and to their reduction in *KMF*.

J. S. Bach, in his *Passacaglia and Fugue in C minor* for organ, has written two movements that are unified by a common theme. The fugue uses as subject the first half of the passacaglia motive. It is no mean feat to expose thoroughly a thematic idea twenty times in as many variations and then proceed to use it still further without giving the listener an overdose. The differences in the treatment, in each movement, help to overcome this difficulty. In the passacaglia, the theme remains in the bass except for a few variations. In the ensuing fugue, however, it appears imitatively among the several voices; episodes in which the subject does not appear even in fragmentary form provide a degree of relief and help ensure our appetite to hear further subject entries.

The passacaglia motive is eight measures long. Small alterations in rhythm (as in variation 5), in imitation of the motive used in the upper voices (variation 9), and as the lowest note in an arpeggio (variations 14–15) are exceptional.[1]

In a passacaglia, as in any variation form, there is danger that the variations may appear to have an arbitrary order. To avoid that danger, Bach writes his twenty variations in four groups (5+5+5+5) in which there is changing intensity rather than a plateau. Tension mounts in the first two groups; in the third, reduced texture and omission of organ pedals (in variation 11) assist a new growth in intensity which drops again, noticeably in variations 14–15, where upward-cascading arpeggios provide lightness and relief from the previous polyphony. The final group of five variations reintroduce the motives previously used, in a texture that combines polyphonic and homophonic elements. The final variation has a very thick texture (five voices) in which the lines having sixteenth-notes appear to reach a point of such tension that they are just capable of trembling within the narrow range of a third. The

1. See *KMF*, Example 16.6.

last beat elides with the first beat of the fugue, to provide continuity and to prevent the dissipation of pent-up energy that would have taken place had there been separation.

We enter a quite different musical world when we hear Mozart's *String Quintet in G minor,* K. 516, the second movement, where a very tightly knit structure conveys sentiments of remarkable poignancy and personal intimacy without a trace of rhetoric or virtuoso display.

Of particular interest is the Trio. This is based, in an easygoing and seemingly effortless way, on the codetta of the Menuetto. Quite simply, the Trio appears to grow out of the Menuetto rather than to follow it.

Example 10.1 *Mozart,* String Quintet in G minor, *K. 516, second movement. The end of the Menuetto and the beginning of the Trio.*

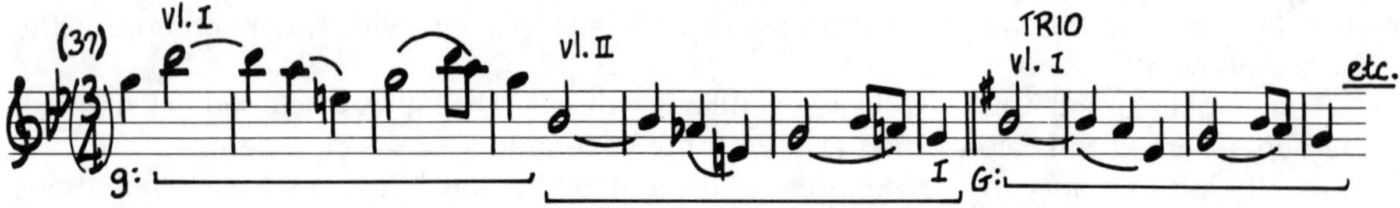

The codetta that terminates the Menuetto is a *twofold* extension in mm. 37–43, compared with the *single* postcadential extension that ends part a^1 in mm. 10–13.

Example 10.2 Ibidem, *mm. 10–13*.

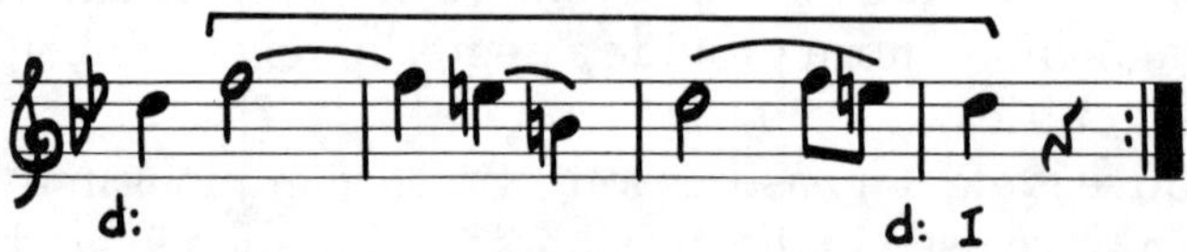

The Trio thus takes up the idea of development by means of varied repetition and continues it to remarkable lengths in a variety of ways, even to the point of employing it again in the codetta of the Trio.

Example 10.3 Ibidem, *Trio, part one* (c^1).

Parts *d* and c^2 continue with this motive, *d* introducing stretto-like imitation in a more polyphonic texture than that observed in c^1. (For analysis of the complete work, see *KMF*, Example 14.4.)

The development section of the first movement of Brahms's *Symphony No. 2 in D major,* if not the most extended of our four illustrations, is certainly the most complex.[2] Its five parts treat in various ways the first theme almost exclusively. The neighboring-tone motive *a* and the chord-outline motive *b* are the chief building blocks.

Example 10.4 *Brahms,* Symphony No. 2 in D major, *first movement. Motives* a *and* b *as presented in mm. 1–5.*

Modulatory scheme, texture, contrapuntal devices, sequence, varied combinations of previous disparate material, and the like, all contribute to making the five parts unified within themselves and distinct from their neighbors.

Part one (mm. 183–205) abandons sharp keys and moves from F major to C minor, using elements of *a* and *b* homophonically, and overlaps the beginning of part two.

Part two (mm. 204–224) moves from C minor (three flats) to E major (four sharps), in a quasi-fugal development of the second phrase (mm. 6–8) against a quasi-countersubject in running eighths.

Part three (mm. 224–246) is tonally stable, moving only from E minor to G major. Motive a^1 is treated sequentially and imitatively, in the original values and in diminution.

Part four (mm. 246–281) is somewhat more active tonally, moving from G to F major. Elements of the principal theme combine with the transition theme of mm. 44–46 and a pattern used earlier in the development (mm. 187–190) in a sequence of largely non-functional harmonies.[3]

2. See *KMF*, pages 280–282.
3. See harmonic structure of mm. 246–281 in *KMF*, page 281. The manner of treatment of the diverse materials is demonstrated here also.

Part five (mm. 282–301) is the retransition and largely an expansion of D:V, as one might expect. Despite the relative tonal stability, compared to the tonal uncertainties of part four, the materials and treatment are similar to that part, which suggests that the two parts should be coupled in thinking of the overall design. Dense texture and intense polyphony create the climax of the movement in this part, which then quietly overlaps with the beginning of a considerably compressed recapitulation of the first theme.[4]

Other factors too numerous to list in detail should be considered as one studies the score. Dynamics (whether at a constant level, whether *pp* or *ff*, crescendo or diminuendo) play an important role in the grand sweep of the development section. Instrumentation (full orchestra, separation of choirs, antiphonal procedures, the use of solo winds, orchestration as it relates to changes of dynamics) is another important compositional tool.

Upon first hearing and reading the score of the *Sonata for Two Pianos*, by Stravinsky, the development section appears to have little relationship to the materials of the exposition, though the movement otherwise is very clearly in sonata form. The movement is quite short (ninety-four measures, of which the first thirty-two constitute a repeated exposition), and the twenty-measure development section is behind us before we realize it.

Everything is miniature. Yet there are four distinct parts, of which the first (mm. 33–36) is an outgrowth of the end of the exposition and serves as introduction to what follows.[5]

Example 10.5 *Stravinsky,* Sonata for Two Pianos, *first movement. End of the exposition and beginning of the development section, reduced.*

The next two and one-half measures briefly develop the neighboring tone figure heard in the preceding measures.

Part two (mm. 37–40) combines elements drawn from both principal and second themes. The principal-theme elements are used in a manner similar to that used in part one.

Example 10.6 Ibidem, *second theme of the exposition (beginning); and development (part two), mm. 37–40, reduced.*

4. See *KMF*, page 282.
5. See *KMF*, Example 23.5. And compare Mozart's similar procedure in Example 10.1 of this chapter.

a) Second theme, mm. 17–18.

b) Development, part two (mm. 37–40).

Part three (mm. 41–46) is closely related to part two in substance and treatment, but is more extended and explores new tonal areas (A♭, and D♭).

Part four (mm. 47–52) is the retransition. It uses a dominant pedal point (A♭, which is D♭:V), but since the recapitulation begins (irregularly) in C major, our pedal point turns out to be dominant of the Neapolitan area (♭II) rather than of the tonic.[6] As materials, it uses chiefly the neighboring-tone figure already heard, but now legato, and the tritone figure, somewhat altered. There is considerable rhythmic displacement, which creates doubt and ambiguity respecting the meter. The shadows of uncertainty are then nicely dispelled in the sunshine of bright C major in forthright 2/4 as the recapitulation begins in m. 53.

As previously indicated (page 98), there is a separation between development and recapitulation, rather than close connection. A degree of connection is made, however, in the use of F as chord-third in the D♭ chord that ends the development, and as first note in the melody in the recapitulation, where it is harmonized by C V^7-over-I, which is used both initially (m. 1) and in the closing measures of the coda (mm. 92–94).[7]

Exercise 10.1 *After studying Example 10.5 in this book and Example 23.5 in* KMF, *and after looking at the complete score and hearing the music (recorded or live), compose a new development section for the Stravinsky movement in question. It may be about the same length or slightly longer and should be in the same general style and employ the same motives, with the possible addition of others from the exposition not used by Stravinsky. There should be from three to five parts and a different key scheme.*

The chief motives shown in Example 10.5 never appeared in inversion or close canonic imitation. Explore these possibilities in preliminary sketches.

In advance of the actual musical composition, a tentative diagram showing the important structural details, prepare and alter it as necessary following consultation with the teacher. Following completion and approval of the first musical sketches, write out the complete work and check the diagram to be sure it corresponds. Performance of the whole movement, possibly before or after Stravinsky's original, should prove to be the basis for useful comparison.

---

6. Compare the similar surprise in the Brahms *Sonata for Violin and Piano*, mentioned on page 101.
7. This use of V^7-over-I should not be confused with polytonality. This device is hardly new. An extended example occurs in the measures preceding the principal theme, second statement, in Beethoven's *Leonore overtures No. 2* and *No. 3*. See also Chopin's *Berceuse*, Op. 57.

Exercise 10.2 *Choose another work, of any period, in compound or extended ternary form, and rewrite the middle section. Pay special attention to the* B *section as development of material from* A, *where this was not the case in the original work. You may wish to use Example 10.3 as a model. Write a brief essay to accompany the composition, explaining what you have done and why you think it is effective.*

Exercise 10.3 *Write a compound ternary form* (aba+cdc+aba) *using original materials, in which you attempt to exploit development procedures to a high degree throughout. Be careful to provide contrast, and do not permit an excess of repetition to render the form unclear. Explain your work in a brief essay.*

11. Composing a Medium-Length Homophonic Work

The term *medium-length form* does not admit to precise definition. It denotes both length and complexity. In Chapter 10, we made reference to a Stravinsky movement in sonata form, a structure that one normally regards as a large form; but because this movement is quite brief and the complexity of its parts not very great, it qualifies as a medium-length form.

The small two- and three-part forms discussed in *KMF* and in the present text consist of units made up of phrases and periods and their extensions. Compound forms, such as the Minuet-and-Trio or Scherzo-and-Trio, or their counterpart structure *aba*+*cdc*+*aba* in a slow movement, certainly qualify as medium-length forms. Insofar as this form was used compositionally in connection with the readings in Chapter 10, the student has already written a medium-length work, but of course there are other types, as we shall see later.

A rondo form may be regarded as "small" if its components are only a phrase or period in length, and if it is part of a larger movement.[1] A rondo may be regarded as medium-length if it is a complete movement and goes beyond the miniature proportions found in the small rondo. In contrast, a large rondo would undoubtedly be of the sonata-rondo type, with extensive use of development procedures.[2]

Sonatina form is sonata form without a development section, and, if its proportions are moderate, a composition with this form would fit our definition. If it is expanded by interpolated developments, as in the finale of Brahms's *Symphony No. 1 in C minor*, the description "medium-length" is inappropriate.

A repertory of medium-length forms might include the following: 1) compound binary or ternary form, in slow or fast tempo; 2) large *ABA* other than compound ternary;[3] 3) rondo

1. See the *B* part of the third movement (mm. 29–60) of Brahms's *Sonata No. 1 in G major for Violin and Piano;* the form of this portion of the movement is itself a small rondo, *ababa*. The movement as a whole is an *ABACA* form. See also the discussion in *KMF*, page 218, and the illustration (Example 21.2) on pages 221–222.
2. See *KMF*, chapters 22 and 24.
3. See, for example, Debussy's *Prelude to the Afternoon of a Faun*, where the *abcd*+*ef* that makes up A^1 is not matched in A^2 except for the prevailing key (E), and *that* is rather vague.

forms *ABABA, ABACA,* or *ABACABA* or slight modifications of these[4], but without the use of development procedures that turn the form into the larger sonata-rondo; 4) sonatina form (without development); 5) compressed or miniature sonata form;[5] 6) variation form, where the theme itself is a small part-form; and 7) combinations of the above.[6]

In the pages that follow, we shall return to the procedure used in earlier chapters, by composing a work and commenting on the compositional process as we go. At the end of the chapter, there are composition exercises, or perhaps one should refer to them as "suggestions for compositions" with the understanding that readers have the option of creating their own plans and then following them wherever they may lead. We hope that, as we get farther along, beginning composers will assert their ideas with increasing freedom from exterior controls, as the inner controls become more and more reliable.

Table 11.1 *Precompositional considerations for a medium-length homophonic work.*

MEDIUM	Oboe and cello.
STYLE	Pandiatonic in certain parts, chromatic in others.
FORM	Modified rondo: *ABACBA*+coda, in which the second and third *A*-parts are increasingly shorter than the initial *A*, with the coda based on *C*.[7]
MOTIVES	A repeated-note figure, and a three-note figure of consecutive fourths.
LENGTH	Part *A*(12 measures) + *B*(10) + *A*(10) + *C*(12) + *B*(10) + *A*(8) + *Coda*(8)=70
TEMPO, METER	Slow, 2/4.
MOOD, CHARACTER	*A*-parts quasi-improvisatory, arioso. *B*-parts lyrical, tempo giusto. *C*-part, dramatic, rhetorical. The *C*-based coda to be similar, but with "flashbacks" of *A* and *B*.
RANGE	Wide in *A*, narrow in *B*, wildly contrasting in *C*.
DYNAMICS	From *mf-f* in *A*, *mf-p* in *B*, and *f-ff* in *C*; mixed in the coda.
CLIMAX	Given the above, it should be in *C*. A secondary climax in the coda.

4. See *KMF*, Chapter 22 ("Altered Rondo Forms").
5. See *KMF*, examples 23.2 and 23.5.
6. See the second movement of Stravinsky's *Octet for Wind Instruments,* which combines variation and rondo. Stylized "popular" forms (dances or a march) alternate with the unvarying rondo theme.
7. See Brahms's use of this procedure (each succeeding *A*-part shorter than the preceding) in his *Sonata in A major for Violin and Piano,* third movement.

With this blueprint we can begin, remembering always that, given good reason for doing so, we may alter some of the details as we proceed.

Example 11.1 *Composing a medium-length rondo for oboe and cello.*

Given our various premises, we rule the bar lines needed for the twelve-measure A^1. Since the style is homophonic, one line at the most may be melodic; the other should be accompanimental. Simultaneous rhythms in block chords may be effective in assuring homophony.

The twelve measures should be subdivided. We decide arbitrarily on 5+5, with a two-measure extension. The key, which should be predetermined, is G. The melody line begins in the oboe, then transfers to the cello. A^1 is pandiatonic.

Inverting the motivic fourths, the cello begins with a quadruple-stop using the open strings. The tonality is somewhat ambiguous, with C and G having almost equal claim to "title." Triplets and sixteenths join ties over bar lines to weaken the meter and aid the sense of free improvisation. Motion in the accompanying instrument is reduced to minimize any contrapuntal competition.

Occasional scale lines provide contrast to the fourths. We try to balance slurred notes with staccato. Left-hand pizzicato in the cello (+) on open strings, and natural harmonics (°) provide color contrast. In mm. 9–10, the consecutive down bows and fingered tremolos offer idiomatic opportunity for the cello, contrast to the sustained notes in the oboe.

The end of A^1 in the key of D is not connected directly with B^1, a lyrical, middle-register, chromatic section that is more clearly homophonic than A^1. The pizzicato intervals and chords help provide contrast to A^1 also.

We subdivide the ten measures as: 3½+4½ (to avoid 4+4 symmetry) plus a two-measure retransition to A^2.

We write the oboe line first, starting on E♭ as the new tonic, a half-step above D (the end of part A^1). We allow the line to meander downward, using whole- and half-steps, to the midpoint, G. The second phrase begins on low E♭, and wends its way up in a modified inversion of the previous descent, to E♮, a half-step higher than our starting point, which is consistent with our plan to dissolve the section rather than end on a cadence; as the highest point in the line, it provides tension useful for the retransition.

The cello part features repeated tones, largely in intervals; but triple-stops occur in the climactic second phrase. Although accompanimental in nature, it borrows the stepwise-motion idea from the oboe, notably where the latter has long notes or rests, to take up the rhythmic slack. The sequentially designed retransition leads directly to A^2 (mm. 23–32).

A^2 is, as preplanned, two measures shorter than A^1. We begin by compressing and modifying the two first measures (compare mm. 23–24 with mm. 1–2). Thereafter, the measures correspond closely, with only small changes. Mm. 25 and 4 are similar in substance, but there is octave transposition in the oboe part, and the cello part is slightly more active. In m. 26, we invert both the intervals and the direction of the line in the oboe part; the cello's variation in m. 26 can be explained as a continuing sequence of m. 25.

Mm. 29–30 in the oboe line are a compression of the materials of mm. 8–10, with oboe and cello exchanging materials in m. 29 to permit the oboe to be more active prior to its cadence in m. 31. The aforementioned compression takes care of the second of the two measures we are omitting in A^2. Mm. 31–32 thus compare with mm. 11–12.

In m. 31, the quintuplets, formerly sixteenths, are now eighths; and in m. 32, instead of a D-harmonic that is abruptly terminated, we have a double-stop D (using one of the open strings as well as a "stopped" D) and ties over the bar line, connecting with part C.

In part *C*, we decide to write the cello line first. It is simply an ascending chromatic line with octave displacements, starting with D, and going up to the tritone A♭ at midpoint (m. 38), allowing 1½ measures for each of the paired scale degrees (D♯-E, F-G♭, G-A♭). The second half (mm. 39–44) uses the same procedure for the remaining tritone within the octave (A♭-D), borrowing the figuration from mm. 34–36 in mm. 40–42. The closing measures (43–44) lead to the restatement of *B*.

Now, writing the oboe part, we use a *descending* chromatic line, in contrary motion to that of the cello, but the interval-groups starting in m. 34 are of one-measure duration, rather than 1½. The relationship between the two lines, as a result, depends upon the accidental coincidences—a quasi-aleatory procedure. We do try to control the rhythmic balance, and so achieve a counterpoint of sorts. We try to avoid symmetry and repetition. There are, however, a number of symmetrical rhythms (triplets and quintuplets). Mm. 40–44 compress the line of 33–39 and prepare us for part B^2, in m. 44 in rhythmic unison with the cello, *piano*.

* Use different fingering for ♪ and ♪. It does not matter if one of the C's is a microtone out of tune.

Part B^2 (mm. 45–54) in essence is a restatement of B^1 (13–22). The chief differences are in the placement of the lines, which have been exchanged in double counterpoint, and in the use of eighth-note triplets instead of even eighths or sixteenths.

Since the oboe cannot literally repeat the cello's double- and triple-stops, the intervals are heard consecutively rather than simultaneously. (We considered using multiphonics, then rejected the idea.)

A measure-for-measure comparison is helpful in exploring the variation procedures. Relief from an excessive number of triplets is achieved in mm. 48–49 and 53–54.

As in B^1, we attain a modest climax near the close; and there is, after that climax, a retransition to A^3. Keeping in mind the oboist's need for breathing points, we have allowed the oboe to rest during most of the retransition. We had already seen to it that there were numerous short rests sprinkled throughout B^2. The cello line, which had been arco in (mm. 21–22, is now pizzicato.

A^3, we decided earlier, is to be an eight-measure compression of A^1. We draw the bar lines first of all.

It occurs to us that we can help to relate A^3 to B^2 by again using the process of exchange of parts. Mm. 55–59, thus, are substantially a double-counterpoint restatement of mm. 1–5. A few changes of rhythm may be observed, along with alterations made in the interest of idiomatic writing for the instruments. The cello, for instance, makes much use of open strings, as in the arpeggios and arpeggiated chords of mm. 58–59. Pizzicato is used only in m. 55, where it serves as connecting link with B^2, and in m. 62, where it doubles the tonic (G) heard in the oboe.

Most of the middle of A^1 is omitted in A^3. The closing measures (60–62) are related to the closing measures of A^1, but we alter the pitches in order to effect an unambiguous cadence on the tonic.

The coda begins with the oboe echoing the repeated cello notes of m. 62.

But again deciding to compose the important bass line first, we attend to the cello part. Using G as a tonic pedal point, the line ascends chromatically, an idea we borrow from part *C*, but we avoid the tension-creating changes of color (col legno, snap pizzicato, etc.). The repeated-note idea of m. 63 returns in m. 67.

The rising line in sixteenths is "lifted" directly from B^1 (mm. 17–18), the triple-stops from mm. 18–19. The closing progression, E major chord to tonic G, is a substitute for V-I, G♯ serving as enharmonic A♭ (Neapolitan, or ♭II). Tonic in the bass register is saved for the very end.

Returning to the beginning of the coda, we write the oboe part, using a descending chromatic line, once again borrowing the idea from part *C*, in a zigzag course from G to D. The closing measures are a transposed repetition of the oboe line in mm. 19–20, rhythmically displaced and adjusted to end on the tonic. The ascent from F♯ to G at the close is, nicely, in contrary motion to the G♯ to G♮ in the cello part.

Before turning to composition exercises, it would be well to examine the extent to which the concepts discussed in chapters 9 and 10 have been applied in the example just completed.

Extension is most clearly observed in the coda, largely a prolongation of the tonic G. The contrasting parts, *B* and *C*, terminated with brief retransitions that led through their stepwise motion and/or motivic figure directly into the following *A* part.

Part A^1 was deliberately separated from B^1, but A^2 and A^3 are (with equal deliberation) closely connected with the parts that follow them.

Hearing the beginnings of A^2 and A^3, (assuming that one hears these as repetitions of A^1), one expects to hear the *complete* part. Surprise enters the picture when the listener realizes that there are omissions and other modifications. The approach to the last chord of the coda is a surprise because of what appears to be a departure from the well-established G as tonic, but the logic behind the unexpected route taken to the final chord is accepted once it is understood, consciously or subconsciously.

Development procedures are somewhat in evidence within each part, but perhaps are most clearly to be observed in A^2 and A^3, which are varied repetitions of A^1. The procedures used have already been described and need not be repeated here, but they might be reviewed by the reader in the context of the present discussion. Contrast in plentiful supply is provided by the opposition of undiluted diatonicism in the *A*-parts to the rather consistent chromaticism in the other parts. If the coda does not reconcile the two styles, which might have been expected from our original premises, at least it does provide a clear, tonal platform to support the chromatic lines above it.

Exercise 11.1 *Using the precompositional assumptions listed in Table 11.1, compose a work that otherwise is completely different from Example 11.1 (which is based upon Table 11.1).*

Exercise 11.2 *Using the parameters listed in column 1 of Table 11.1, indicate in another column a different set of particulars and details. Then proceed to compose, part by part, using the kind of format we employed in Example 11.1—music on the left, comments on the right. If you are unsure of the way you are carrying out your decisions, check with your instructor for advice as you proceed.*

Exercise 11.3 *Prepare a table of considerations similar to Table 11.1 but not necessarily including the identical parameters—keep those you regard as useful and necessary and add any that are helpful. After you have completed both columns, consult your instructor for suggestions or approval. Then proceed in the usual manner. Completed work, as always, should be performed and heard by the composer. Considered judgment by one's peers is an important adjunct to that of one's teacher and a valuable part of the "business" of learning how to cultivate an audience, even if not necessarily how to please or entertain it.*

Exercise 11.4 *Write a medium-length composition utilizing one of the structures other than rondo as enumerated on page 110. Follow the procedures suggested for the exercises above.*

Exercise 11.5 *Combine elements of two or more forms, such as the one described in footnote 6 on page 110. Prepare an outline or diagram of your plans, which should be reviewed and approved before you commence work.*

12. Composing a Medium-Length Polyphonic Work

In Chapter 4, we reviewed the distinctions between polyphonic compositions that are based upon *imitative* and *non-imitative* counterpoint. We should refresh our memories by looking again at the composed illustrations, Examples 4.1 and 4.2. The polyphonic devices described in *KMF* (Chapter 10) and utilized in Chapter 4 of the present text need no elaboration at this point.

But it would be well to consider the forms and styles discussed in *KMF*, chapters 16–20, many of which lend themselves to the needs of polyphonic compositions of medium length. The ostinato-type works illustrated in *KMF*, Chapter 16, are large-scale rather than medium-length, except for the Purcell and Bach works mentioned in Example 16.5. The Bach *Goldberg Variations*, a theme with thirty variations, is another work that is large-scale (see *KMF*, Example 17.4). Inventions and fugues (see *KMF*, chapters 18–19) are almost always of medium length—and exceptions might be made of double and triple fugues, which because of complexity and duration qualify as large-scale. Similarly, chorale variations (*KMF*, Chapter 20) are medium-length in most instances, though one based upon a two- or three-phrase melody without much elaboration might qualify as "short." If the procedure is used in a long movement, as in Bartók's *Piano Concerto No. 3*, or in several movements of a cantata for chorus (or solo voice) and orchestra, or in a chorale partita for organ solo, then clearly a large-scale design has been conceived by the composer.

Because imitative counterpoint is thoroughly documented in *KMF* and widespread in the standard literature, and because of new interest in our own time in the possibilities of non-imitative counterpoint, we elect in this chapter to elaborate upon the string trio of Example 4.2, using that one-part composition as the basis for a medium-length work of three parts, featuring non-imitative polyphony, an *ABC* form in which *C*(rather than introduce new material) combines elements of *A* and *B*.

Our design is a blend of 1) traditional *ABA* form, which today is difficult to carry off without its seeming too obvious, especially in A^2, and 2) *ABC* form, a through-composed form in which unity is achieved, usually, by means of motivic repetition (see *KMF*, Example 25.12).

Example 4.2 has a degree of roundness and complexity that makes it less than ideally suited to serve as the *A*-part of our *ABC* form. We decide, therefore, to try to use it as the *C*-part. If *C* is to combine elements of *A* and *B*, then it follows that we shall have to abstract certain elements from *C*, contrasting ideas that may be used separately at first in *A* and *B*. Logically speaking, therefore, *A* and *B* materials are derived by a process of *analysis*, though the evident result to the listener, in part *C*, is a procedure of *synthesis*.

The example shown in Chapter 4 is twenty-two measures long. We decide, somewhat (but not altogether) arbitrarily, to make the *B*-part the shortest of the three, and *A* of a length in between *B* and *C*. The reasoning behind this decision derives from our conception of *C* as a mixture and a development of *A* and *B*, and time is needed for this development to take place. So, it is decided that *B* shall have seventeen measures, *A*, twenty measures, making them shorter than *C* by five and two measures, respectively.

Example 4.2, our *C*-part-to-be, is a mirror or retrograde form. We decide to use this idea in part *A*, but not in *B*. Thus, it will be one of the elements in *C* derived from *A*. Furthermore, in *C*, there is much contrast between arco and pizzicato. We decide, once more in arbitrary manner but with a view toward realizing our formal objective, that *A* will be arco and *B*, pizzicato, so that the use of both in *C* will further help the listener recognize that in part three there are elements from parts one and two. Finally, we shall limit triplets and quintuplets to part *B*, so that their use, together with regular notes in *C*, is heard as a mixture of *A* and *B*. Part three will, as a result of these decisions, be the climactic part of the whole work.

Example 12.1 *Composing a medium-length movement for string trio, in non-imitative style,* ABC-*form.*

After ruling the bar lines of the first six measures of our twenty-measure *A*-part, and furthering our plan to base *A* on materials of *C*, we first write out the opening six measures of the viola part, con sordino, deriving our notes from the violin part of mm. 1–6 in Example 4.2. We have eliminated the triplet and septuplet rhythms, and made the line more vocal in style. Crescendo and diminuendo also are new features. The pizzicato triple-stop is replaced by a single note, an artificial harmonic.

The violin has a similar adaptation of the cello part of mm. 1–6. Addition of an open A-string as a pedal point provides tonal stability. The cello line is based upon the viola part of mm. 1–3. All parts are arco, con sordino, and contrasting in materials.

We continue part *A* by further use of the quasi-double counterpoint that appeared in mm. 1–6. The viola part (mm. 7–10) is based upon the violin part of mm. 7–10 of part *C* (see pages 39–40); the violin part in these measures is derived from the cello part in the same manner; the cello part, from the viola. This is easily demonstrated in the following chart:

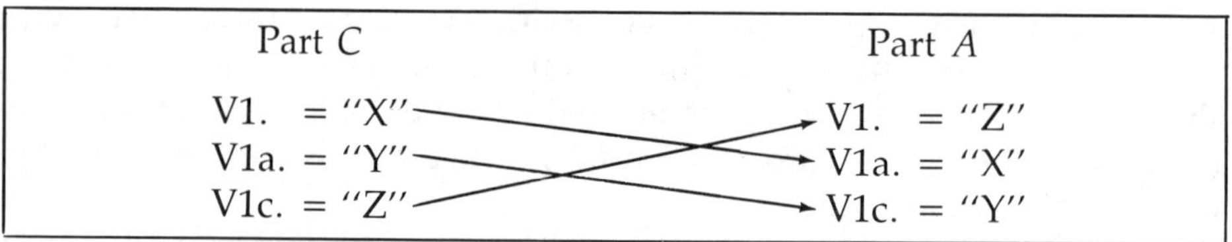

There is a gradual crescendo to the climax in mm. 10–11, which marks also the turning point in our mirror form. The lines pursue their independent course, with our maximum attention given to rhythm contrast, minimum attention to harmonic coincidences.

The next six measures continue the retrograde motion begun in m. 11. Thus, mm. 13–18 correspond to mm. 3–8. We make a few small alterations in the interest of rhythmic balance or motion. The previous crescendo now must be diminuendo. We raise the dynamic level in the viola part somewhat, in the interest of greater dynamic intensity. Mm. 19–20, retrograding mm. 1–2, bring part *A* to a close. There is no transition to *B*, and we make no attempt to connect the two parts. Rests permit the mutes to be removed.

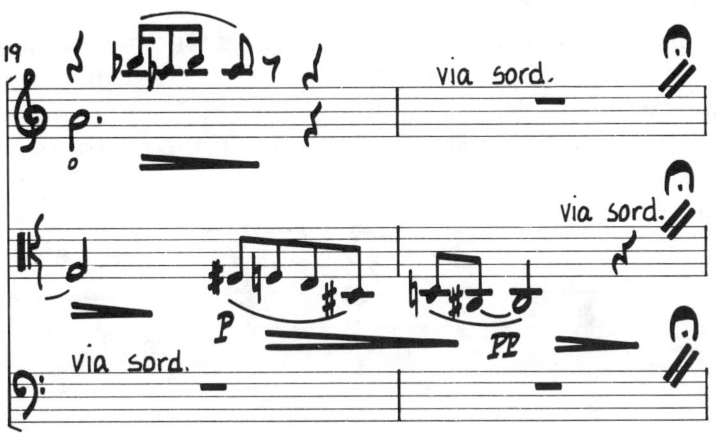

Before beginning part *B*, we formulate our "strategy." First of all, stimulated by the double counterpoint in part *A*, we decide to employ *triple* counterpoint in part *B*. The chart below shows how the lines are exchanged in this procedure.

	A	*B*	*C*
Violin	"Z"	"Y"	"X"
Viola	"X"	"Z"	"Y"
Cello	"Y"	"X"	"Z"

In addition, we decide that part *B* is to grow out of *A* in line but *not* in rhythm. As previously mentioned, we avoided triplets, quintuplets, and septuplets in *A*, but we shall use them exclusively in *B*—with the possible exception of some long notes (half- and whole-notes).

The lines, for further contrast, are transposed at the tritone (up or down), and pizzicato replaces arco; the mutes have been removed.

The first ten measures of part *B* (21–30) will be based on the first ten measures of *A* (1–10), but the balance of *B* (mm. 31–37) is to be an extended transition, at first growing out of the immediately preceding measures, and then anticipating the opening measures of part *C*. We will attempt to make a smooth connection between *B* and *C*, and at the same time make clear exactly where part *C* begins. During those last measures, we must allow rests in order for the performers to once again place the mutes on the bridges of their instruments. For readers to make the connection between parts *B* and *C*, they will have to turn to pages 38–42, where all of *C* appears. Then it will be necessary to review the entire work, to be sure nothing is amiss. It is quite possible that the larger structure will require a coda. If that proves to be so, then we shall write one, altering the very end of *C* if that seems to be desirable.

Just to start things off, we write only the first three measures of part *B* (21–23). All parts are senza sordino and pizzicato, as planned, and transposed a tritone above or below the source in part *C*. The violin plays F♯ and F♮ followed by C-B♭-A♭-G♭, which is derived from the viola's notes C-B followed by F♯-E-D-C. The repetition of the first two notes is retained, but the rhythm is altered; the third measure retains rhythm *and* line. Sharp contrast of dynamics (*p* vs. *ff*) replaces consistent *pp*.

Similarly, the viola part in mm. 21–23 is derived from the cello's notes at the beginning of part *C*, and the cello part is derived from the violin notes.

A pattern of alternation of loud and soft is established, and generally agreed upon in the three string parts. The rhythms are a bit "tricky" to play, but they are for the most part complementary, and largely triplets; the quintuplets of m. 23 are exceptional, and to justify their use, we must endeavor to employ them further in the measures to come.

Mm. 24–26 continue the procedure and style now established.

Mm. 27–30 are a continuation of mm. 24–26; they bring us to the point where parallelism with part *C* stops. There is a general rise in the dynamic level, and an increase in the number of snap pizzicatos. The number of isolated notes appearing on weak fractions increases too, adding to the sense of rising tension. Measure-for-measure examination of the relation of these bars to the corresponding ones in part *C* will reveal the means used to secure variation.

In our transition, m. 31 is a repetition of m. 30, but with exchange of parts: violin line goes to cello, viola to violin, cello to viola. It is all *ff,* and there is greater use of the snap pizzicato. M. 32 repeats 29. The appearance of mm. 29–30 in 31–32 suggests the retrograde procedures in part *C* just ahead. There is exchange of parts similar to that in m. 31. The cello begins the use of *piano,* which continues through m. 35.

In m. 33, there is a repetition of m. 32, but at the tritone, and all parts are now *piano.* Violin and viola play arco instead of pizzicato; the cello continues pizzicato.

In m. 34, in anticipation of m. 1 of part *C* (see Example 4.2), the viola sustains the G and the cello uses the quarter-note quintuplet figure. The violin rests, puts on the mute. (Each instrument is allowed two measures to replace the mute.)

Mm. 34–35 in the cello anticipate the first two measures of part C. In mm. 36–37, the texture thins out to prepare for the entries at the beginning of C. The violin part is taken from m. 5 of part C, and thus anticipates it. The extended C♯ provides connection with part C. The use of quarter-note triplets after the eighth-note triplets is a "built in" ritenuto that is useful in preparing for the quasi–*a tempo* in part C.

The measure numbers of part C (Example 4.2) now should be changed from the old 1–22 to the new ones: 38–59. Part C should be reexamined in the light of its new structural context. Does it work? Are there problems that require rewriting of the music? Is a coda needed? If so, why, and what formal and expressive purpose would it serve? Upon what materials should it be based, and why? If no coda is needed, then we may leave things as they are. As always, the best test of one's efforts is in an actual performance. We may need to change some of the dynamics. Perhaps the tempo is too fast. There may be some notes that are awkward in performance (the string players will make these known to us!) and need substitutes. The performers should have parts that provide cues that show the other parts, particularly where there are rhythmic difficulties. A line with rhythmic cues is a useful supplement to the main part. Generally, this procedure is preferable to the practice of asking all the players to read from the full score, though that may be the lesser evil in an extremely complex score where everybody must know precisely what is happening in all the parts.

Procedures for composing medium-length compositions in *imitative polyphony* are clearly explained in *KMF*, and it is therefore unnecessary to duplicate those materials here. The exercises at the ends of chapters 18 (on invention), 19 (on fugue), and 20 (chorale variation) in *KMF* might very appropriately be attempted at this point. In the usual manner, one should prepare tables, charts and plans before starting the actual compositional work. And an explanatory essay should accompany the music, step by step.

Exercise 12.1 *Compose a medium-length ostinato-type work for organ or two pianos. There should be a five- or six-measure "ground" or ostinato figure, and from twenty to twenty-five "variations" over it. The first statement should be unaccompanied. Attempt some large-scale plans for structure, so that variations come in groups rather than a series of 1+1+1. . . . Prepare advance sketches for approval and a brief essay explaining your compositional procedures.*

Exercise 12.2 *Compose a fugue in which there are three parts. Part one is the exposition and short development; part two utilizes the subject in inversion; part three uses the original subject in stretto. Other devices (diminution and augmentation) are optional. Retrograde should not be used unless the subject lends itself to such treatment.*

Exercise 12.3 *Compose a choral variation in motet or fugal style, in which the chorale appears in augmentation—each phrase heard as the last entry in each group of entries (see* KMF, *examples 20.10 and 20.12 for models).*

Exercise 12.4 *Compose a work using* non-imitative *counterpoint. You may take example 12.1 as a procedural model. You may use three- or four-part form, and the usual preliminary planning should be thought out and approved before you commit notes to paper. A descriptive essay should accompany the music. It might be helpful for each of the several parts to be written and approved before you attempt to complete the entire work. Performance will probably require the copying of solo parts, which should be carefully prepared. Be sure there are enough cues, and of course number all the measures. You should solicit and evaluate the critical observations of the performers in this exercise, as in all your work.*

13. Composing a Medium-Length Work for Accompanied Voice or Vocal Ensemble

Some of the compositional techniques that have special relevance to vocal music have already been illustrated—see examples 2.2 (a short unaccompanied solo vocalise), 6.1 (a work for SATB chorus accompanied by organ), and 7.1 (an accompanied solo song in ternary form). Our interest in the present chapter is in forms more extended than these. Furthermore, we shall attempt to incorporate and demonstrate some of the compositional procedures that have been presented to the reader in the intervening chapters.

A number of characteristic medium-length vocal forms are illustrated in *KMF*, Chapter 25, and might usefully be reviewed at this point: examples 25.7 (a two-part aria), 25.8 (bar form), 25.9 (da capo aria), 25.10 (three-part aria, *ABA*), 25.11 (aria in strophic form, $A^1 A^2 A^3$), and 25.12 (song in through-composed form). Mentioned there, but not illustrated, is the recitativo followed by aria, of which the familiar latter-day counterpart is the verse and chorus—the standard form of twentieth-century Broadway musical comedy.

The first of our two projects to combine vocal and instrumental resources will be a solo song with small instrumental ensemble accompanying. The second will require a mixed chorus (SATB) accompanied by a single instrument. Both works are based upon texts taken from plays by Beaumarchais (in English translation), *The Barber of Seville* and its sequel *The Marriage of Figaro,* masterful comedies that have had some difficulty surviving in their original form thanks to the overwhelming musical settings by Rossini and Mozart.[1]

The solo song is based upon the monologue of Bazile (Basilio in Italian, Basil in English), music master of Rosine, the young ward of Dr. Bartolo, whose attempt to marry Rosine is thwarted by her young lover, Count Almaviva, assisted by Figaro, the barber of Seville. Bazile's ironic remarks on the effectiveness and the irresistibility of calumny are as cutting and as amusing today as they were in his own time (1732–1799).

1. A prior version of *The Barber* by Paisiello was similarly put in the shade by Rossini's definitive adaptation.

> Calumny, sir. You don't realize its effectiveness. I've seen the best of men pretty near overwhelmed by it. Believe me, there's no spiteful stupidity, no horror, no absurd story that one can't get the idle-minded folk of a great city to swallow if one goes the right way about it—and we have some experts here!
>
> [§] First the merest whisper skimming the earth like a swallow before the storm—*pianissimo*—a murmur and it's away sowing the poisoned seed as it goes. Someone picks it up and—*piano piano*—insinuates it into your ear. The damage is done. It spawns, and crawls and spreads and multiplies and then—*rinforzando*—from mouth to mouth it goes like the very Devil.
>
> [§] Suddenly, no one knows how, you see Calumny raising its head hissing, puffing, and swelling before your very eyes. It takes wing, extending its flight in ever-widening circles, swooping and swirling, drawing in a bit here and a bit there, sweeping everything before it, and breaks forth at last like a thunder clap to become, thanks be to Heaven, the general cry, a public *crescendo*, a chorus universal of hate, rage, and condemnation. Who the deuce can resist it?[2]

This text almost cries out for a musical setting. It has a long but single line of development, and grows dynamically from *pianissimo* to *fortissimo*. The words "swallow before the storm—*pianissimo*," with their hissing sibilants, immediately followed by "sowing the poisoned seed as it goes," provide onomatopoeia that is as musical as it is literary. Then we have "hissing, puffing, and swelling" and "swooping and swirling" and the even harsher accents of "hate, rage, and condemnation." As the last line puts it: "Who the deuce can resist it?" And so we try to match wits with Beaumarchais.

The original text is without division into paragraphs. The writer added separations to help make possible a preliminary assessment of the inherent form—the whole thing is too much of a bite to swallow in one piece. The first paragraph is an expanded hosanna to the effectiveness of calumny. Paragraph 2 describes how the mischief begins and then spreads. The final paragraph is a rhapsody on the glorious fulfillment of this devilish behavior, rising in a thunderous crescendo, but ending with a sly, detached, and rather campy question with a double meaning—and no answer.

As in Example 7.1, which also set a prose rather than a poetic text, our next step must be the metricization of the words. Each paragraph has sentences, and these sentences should be clearly distinguishable. The composer must find strong and weak pulses, and determine meter, tempo, and separations between sentences and within sentences. The more specifically musical elements will be determined later.

Example 13.1 *Composing a medium-length work for solo voice and instrumental ensemble based upon the "Calumny" monologue in Beaumarchais's* The Barber of Seville.

First step. We examine the text with a view to determining the metric and the rhythmic properties of the music with which the words are to be associated.

2. From Act 2, *The Barber of Seville,* by Caron de Beaumarchais, translated by John Wood, Penguin Books (1964, reprinted 1976), copyright © 1964, John Wood. Used with permission.

PRESTO

(PARAGRAPH 1)

2/4

(INTRODUCTION) Ca-lum-ny, sir. You don't re-a-lize

its ef-fec-tive-ness. I've seen the best of men

pret-ty near o-ver-whelmed by it. Be-lieve me

there's no spite-ful stu-pi-di-ty, no hor-ror,

no ab-surd sto-ry that one can't get the i-dle-

mind-ed folk of a great ci-ty to swal-low if one goes the

right way a-bout it -- and we have some ex-

perts here! (INTERLUDE)

(PARAGRAPH 2)

First the mer-est whis-per skim-ming the earth like a

swal-low be-fore the storm -- pia-nis-si-mo -- a

70

mur-mur and its a-way sow-ing the poi-soned seed

80

as it goes. 2 Some-one picks it up and -- pia-no

pia-no -- in-sin-u-ates it in-to your ear. 2 The

90

da-mage is done. 2 It spawns, and crawls and

100

spreads and mul-ti-plies and then— rin-for-

zan-do— 1 from mouth to mouth it goes like the

110

ve-ry De-vil. (6) ‖ (6/8)

(INTERLUDE)

(PARAGRAPH 3)

(♩ = ♩. →)

120

Sud-den-ly, no one knows how, you see Ca-lum-ny

rais-ing its head hiss-ing, puff-ing, and swell-ing be-

fore your ve-ry eyes. 1 It takes wing, ex-

130

tend-ing its flight in e-ver wi-den-ing cir-cles,

swoop-ing and swirl-ing, draw-ing in a bit
140
here and a bit there, sweep-ing ev'-ry-thing before it, and breaks forth at last like a thun-der
clap to be-come, thanks be to Hea-ven, the gen'-ral
150
cry, a pub-lic cre-scen-do, a cho-rus u-ni-ver-sal of
161
hate, rage, and con-dem-na-tion. 3 Who the
170
deuce can re-sist it? 6 4
(CODA ......)

Note that we have allowed for an instrumental introduction, two interludes, and a coda. The first and last of these serve as "frame" for the "picture"; the interludes provide a few moments for reflection and for the singer to rest. Paragraph 1 has three internal pauses of about two measures each, for reasons both practical and rhetorical; paragraph 2 has four such pauses; paragraph 3 has three, but they are a bit shorter, except for the highly rhetorical separation prior to the equally rhetorical final question. Paragraph 2 includes some words that are spoken in rhythm rather than sung, and in paragraph 3, the meter changes from 2/4 to 6/8—more to accommodate the larger number of dactylic rhythms (/˘˘) than to change tempo.

The dynamic markings arise naturally from the text. In paragraph 1, except for the opening two sentences, *forte,* there is a gradual rise from *p* to *mf.* With the return to *piano* in the last phrase, the singer should gesture toward the audience! In paragraph 2, we begin *pianissimo* and rise to *forte,* a greater rise than in paragraph 1. The third paragraph should have frequent changes, alternating between *ff* and *pp,* in an atmosphere of near-hysteria, but with mounting tension and longer periods of *ff* near the end. The unanswered question should be *mf;* the singer should wear a grimace on his face.

Second step. We determine instrumentation, type of voice, compositional style, and form.

Instrumentation: flute, horn, cello, and timpani. Woodwind, brass, string, and percussion types provide color contrast and also much-needed contrasts of register. The flute is particularly useful to accompany the words "whisper," "skimming," and "murmur" in paragraph 2. The horn can snarl and grunt, when muted, for the "stupidity" and "horror" in paragraph 1, the "hate," "rage," and "condemnation" of paragraph 3. The cello is multi-faceted: it can be mockingly lyrical, it can veritably spit out its snap pizzicatos in scorn, and it can slide and slither where the text "spawns, and crawls and spreads . . . like the very Devil." Timpani provide bombast when needed, mysterious glissandos (by use of the pedal), not to mention a "thunder clap"—and they of course can add generously to the "public crescendo" near the end.

The voice should be a dramatic baritone, possibly a high bass-baritone, with Mephistophelian and Machiavellian overtones, somewhat like that needed to sing the title role in Boito's *Mefistofele*, or like Chaliapin in Moussorgsky's *The Song of the Flea*. A two-octave range is demanded, low F to high F.

Compositional style: a somewhat diatonicized twelve-tone procedure in the manner of the author's opera *Amerika*, after the novel by Franz Kafka. It will need to have flexibility, to be more chromatic in the highly intense passages, more diatonic in the less dramatic portions of the text. And the form, given the structure of the text, will necessarily have to be through-composed. Motives to provide unity should be devised. Instrumental extensions, interludes, etc., may be related to each other to provide additional cohesion.

The next step is to determine our row and variants. Following that, we may prepare the musical sketches, perhaps beginning this time with the introduction, instead of leaving that for last.

Third step. We set forth the original row **O**, the inversion **I**, retrograde **R**, retrograde of the inversion **RI**, and inversion of the retrograde **IR**.[3]

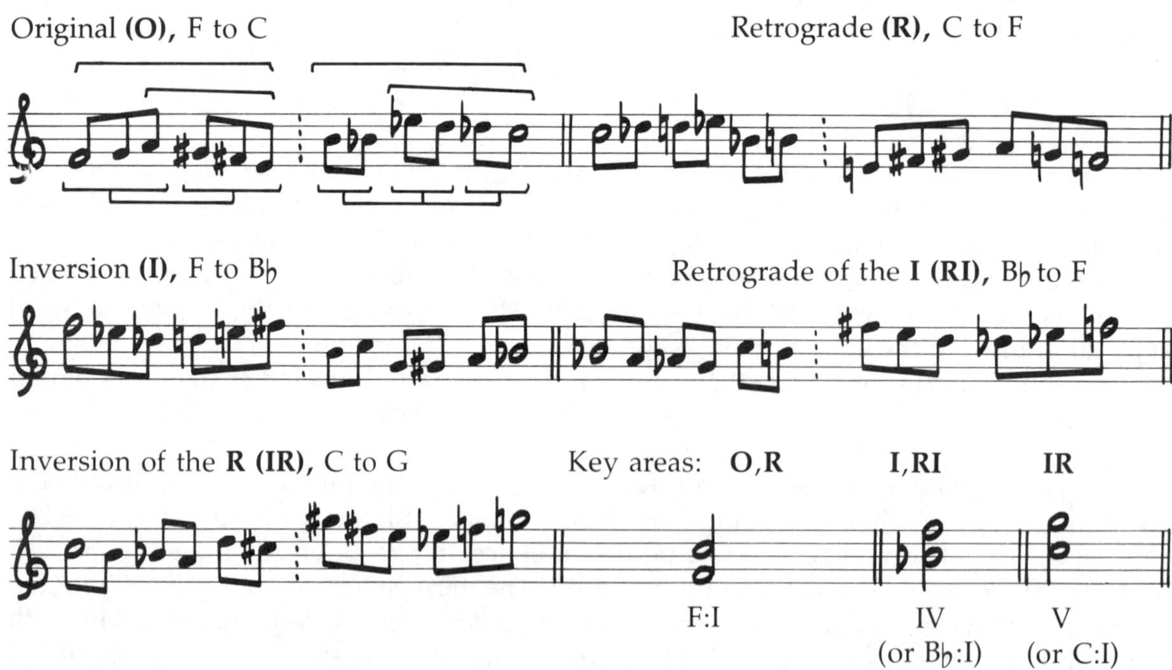

3. Most twelve-tone theorists regard **IR** simply as a transposition of **RI**, which it is. But since we shall not otherwise use transposition, it makes a useful fifth alternative. As the analysis shows, **O** and **R** are largely tonic (I) because of the emphasis on F and C; **I** and **RI** are subdominant; and **IR** provides the complementary dominant area (V).

Analysis of the row and its variants reveals that the original (**O**) is grouped 6+6, fairly standard practice in twelve-tone procedure; that the first six are rather diatonic in character and largely made up of whole-steps; and that the second six are chromatic and largely of half-steps. The subgroups are 3+3 and 2+2+2, as shown by beams and small brackets, but there is a secondary relationship between the last four of each group of six, namely the outline of a tetrachord (A-G♯-F♯-E and E♭-D-D♭-C), if one admits the distinction between a diatonic and a chromatically compressed tetrachord. Strategically placed perfect intervals (fifths or fourths) permit the ear to hear the functional relationship of I-IV or V-I. The row, as a whole, goes from F to C, as if from F:I to F:V (or F:I to C:I).

The retrograde (**R**) is the same but in reverse; the inversion (**I**) is a vertical mirror of **O**; **RI** is a horizontal mirror of **I**, and **IR** a vertical mirror of **R**.

White note-heads are used to show beginnings and ends of rows, to reveal more clearly the tonic-dominant polarity, and they show up again in the summary explanation of the basis for considering key areas.

Fourth step. After ruling the bar lines, we compose the six-measure introduction. The original row (**O**) appears in mm. 1–4 in the unaccompanied line that is doubled at the octave. In m. 1, the quadruple-stop of the cello[4] plus low kettledrum note provides an arresting start.

Example 13.1 *"Calumny," song for solo voice, flute, horn, cello, and timpani.*

In mm. 5-7, the texture thickens and the intensity increases. The retrograde (**R**) is used here. Notes 8–11 appear to be "missing" in the main line (doubled at first in the horn, then in the cello) but they may be found as counterpoint material in the other lines.

By use of **O** and **R**, we are able to begin and end on F, our chosen tonic.

4. The G and one of the A's are played on open strings; the F and the other A are played on the C and D string, respectively. It may prove more effective to eliminate the open A, because the chord may then be played more easily without changing bow position and because the finger stopping the other A may touch the open A and prevent it from sounding as written.

The voice enters on the tonic and continues with the **O**-row to m. 24, accompanied by the instruments, which present the entire **O** in the course of mm. 8–11. Starting with m. 12, the instruments use the **R**-row, but now more homophonically, that is, as chords.

To prevent the runaway appearance of all twelve tones at once, and to take advantage of the time-tested principle of common-tone connection of adjacent chords, we use notes E♭ and B♭ as common tones in the otherwise different chords in mm. 13 and 14. M. 13 is a rearrangement (and inversion) of the chord in m. 12. The notes E and B in mm. 14–15 mark the point where **O** and **R** meet, while going in opposite directions. The cello notes nicely assist the singer to find his pitches, a practical concern one should remember when writing for voice.

The doubled, unaccompanied melodic line returns in mm. 16–17, during the singer's brief pause.

In mm. 17–18, the timpani B doubles the singer's pitch; the tritone leap is our old friend the *diabolus in musica,* which is appropriate to the devilry of the text.

Mm. 19–20 use **R** 1–4 and 3–6, respectively.

We composed first mm. 7–24 with the

solo line complete, and only afterward did we write the accompaniment. The vocal part backtracks in mm. 21–22, repeating the notes E♭ and D of mm. 19–20, a necessity in order to allow us to end on C (note 12 of **O**), but a virtue as well, since we have a legitimate reason for our economy of resource. We tried, throughout, to accent appropriately the emphatic syllables of the text: ef-*fect*-iveness, *best*, and over-*whelmed*.

We tend to place chords where they do not interfere with the words, thus allowing them to be heard and at the same time providing a rhythmic counterpoint.

In mm. 21–24, the voice may not be "over-whelmed" by the canonic imitation, but at least there is a threat to the audibility of the text. Timpani repeat B and F in modified echo of mm. 17–18. In m. 24, **O** ends in the voice, **R** in the instruments.

This was a rather large step, number four! We have reached just about the midpoint of part one (paragraph one). Before continuing, we should review what we have done. We have used only **O** and **R** in the accompaniment, only **O** in the vocal part. Logic suggests that we balance this in the second half of part one. I suggest we try to use only **R** in the vocal part, mirroring our procedure in the first half. The instruments will continue to use **O** and **R**. We conserve our resources, as it were, and plan to use **I**, **RI**, and **IR** later on. The intensity should rise somewhat, but not too much. Again, we must save the real climax for later.

Fifth step. After ruling the bar lines for mm. 25–47, we write the vocal line, then the accompaniment. We shall take care of the instrumental bridge of mm. 48–49 (the final clause of the text) and the interlude in a later step.

Note repetitions help provide tonal security for the singer, and permit a degree of stress when there is a change of scale degrees. High notes provide extra stress. The **R**-row "expires" on the F in m. 41, so we repeat it immediately, but this time we "save" the last three notes of **R** (A-G-F) for the final clause of the sentence in mm. 50–53.

The slightly meandering course of the **O**-row, 1–12, in mm. 25–28, is shown by numbers in small circles. A number of overlaps and repetitions may be observed.

In mm. 25–28, the accompaniment style and texture change, to suggest murmuring and whispering, somewhat impressionistically. The **O**-row appears in its entirety in these measures. The dynamics are *piano* except for the muted snarl in the horn.

The next four measures counterpoint the notes 1–4 of **R** in the voice against the complete **R** in the instruments. We continue the textural style of mm. 25–28. The horn and timpani, glissando, imitate each other and support the voice.

In mm. 33–36, against notes 4–6 of **R** in the voice, we hear all of **O** in the accompaniment. There are fewer tremolos now, and more single notes. The flute exploits flutter-tongue; the cello alternates between pizzicato and arco; and the timpani roll and slide while continuing the support of the vocal line. We resist the temptation to overindulge in illustrating the words "horror" and "absurd."

The next four measures (37–40) find us continuing the cello and timpani tremolos; single notes become more insistent. The horn's hand-stopped (muted) notes, *sf*, reflect the text. Repeated tones provide some background stability for the rather long sentence, which must be allowed to register in one's consciousness. The voice uses **R** (6–11), the instruments likewise, but complete (1–12).

In mm. 41–44, we borrow rhythm and texture from mm. 7–10, but use **R** (rather than **O**), notes 1–6. This procedure helps prevent the texture from becoming further involved in textural complexity (we wish to save that for later), and also assists us in our quest for structural unity. The horn glissando may resemble the reverse of a swallow, suggested in the text, but it is more effective and idiomatic than a descending glissando.

The next three measures close the sentence, except for the ironic phrase that is tagged on to the end. Notes 5–12 of **R** are used in three chords (texture and rhythm borrowed from mm. 12–14) each with two common tones, thus: 5, 6, 7, 8—7, 8, 9, 10—9, 10, 11, 12. Mm. 48–49 are extensions of the last chord, forming a brief interruption before the closing phrase of the paragraph (mm. 50–53), which is accompanied only by timpani and horn, with a few knowing winks from the cello, col legno.[5]

5. The dry col legno sounds in the cello underscore the drollery of the sung text at this point.

Sixth step. This is a short one. We complete the instrumental bridge already begun in m. 48 and set the balance of the text of paragraph 1, plus the interlude of six measures. We have already indicated our plans for the final phrase of text. For the interlude, we decide, in the interest of formal unity (much needed in this through-composed structure) to borrow heavily from the introduction. However, we have also decided to use the inverted row (**I**) and its inversion (**RI**) in part two, rather than **O** and **R**. We therefore prepare for that by using the **I**-row in the interlude. Once more—bar lines first, then the notes.

The rather ironic text in mm. 50–52 is set to the last three notes of the **R**-row, in a deliberately low register. The instruments still further prolong the last *four* notes of **R**, assisting the vocalist's pitch and at the same time providing some appropriate coloristic effects. Flutter-tongue, previously heard only in the flute, appears now also in the horn. M. 53 is simply an extension.

The interlude, mm. 54–59 (really to the downbeat of m. 60), uses the inverted row (**I**), as previously decided. The parallelism of mm. 54–55 to mm. 1–2 is quite evident, if one allows for the use of triplets instead of even eighths, and the use of **I** instead of **O**. The ensuing four measures (56–59) similarly are based upon 3–6, but the texture is more polyphonic. Downbeats of mm. 60 and 7 correspond in function.

Seventh step. Compose part two. We first write the complete vocal line. Beat one (m. 60) is an elision connecting parts one and two. The notes B♭ and F announce the appearance of **I** and **RI**, the row forms to be used in part two. Since B♭ is both end of the **I**-row and beginning of the **RI**, its elision function is quite clear and "serves notice" that the F-C polarity of part one has been replaced.

Mm. 60–67 are characterized by the presence in the vocal part of the complete **RI**. The accompaniment follows a similar course, but completes the row on the F in m. 64. The cello and flute lines then backtrack to F♯ and between the two of them repeat the second half of **RI**.

The horn notes serve two functions: as imitative development of the two-note figure derived from the flute, and as vocal support. The tremolando sixteenths are a bit of tone painting, to suggest the skimming swallows.

B♭ and F in mm. 66–69 serve as connections, this time between **RI** and the **I**-row that follows. Timpani notes in mm. 66–67 are played on a single drum, of course, and serve as augmented imitation of the last notes in the textual phrase. Since **RI** is now followed by **I**, the notes D♭-E♭-F just heard in the timpani are heard in retrograde when the voice enters in mm. 69–71, a curious instance of double retrograde!

After the *pianissimo* interjection, a verbal use of the interpolation principle, our next phrase unit is mm. 69–75. Here appears the **I**-row, as just indicated, the first half only, in the vocal line. The instruments engage in considerable note repetition, and go a bit farther—to note 8. The low, stopped notes in the horn suggest the "poisoned seed."

Despite the ostensible two-measure break in mm. 76–77, the instruments overlap the sentences by virtue of the coupling in mm. 75–76 and 77–78. Thus, flute and cello provide all of the second half of the **I**-row in mm. 75–76, while timpani continue the B-F♯ tremolo in transfer from the cello, and the horn sounds a sinister low C, a tritone from the voice's F♯.

Mm. 77–80 form a *four*-measure group, if one considers instrumentation and motives, 2+2; but the vocal part suggests a *three*-measure group beginning on m. 78. This structural overlap creates cohesion and, to a degree, added tension. Flute and cello backtrack, using notes 5–10 and 7–10, respectively. Timpani continue the tremolo, almost as a pedal point, and with the horn help the singer find his notes.

The next five measures (81–85) continue the backtracking maneuvers in the row treatment, using notes 6–10, in apparent reluctance to go on to 11 and 12. But this restraint allows us to use more effectively notes 11 and 12 at the end of the sentence, in the voice. Note 11 (A) is buried in the buzzing chord of m. 84, the mild sting of which may suggest the entry of the seed into the ear.

Mm. 86–89 provide a radical change in texture, again illustrative of the text. **RI** is used here, with notes 1–4 in m. 86, and all twelve in the remaining three measures. The table shows how the twelve tones are distributed:

Fl.: 1, 4, 7, 10 (·/.)
Vlc.: 2, 5, 8, 11 (·/.)
Hr.: 3, 6, 9, 12 (·/.)

The singer's rests, particularly in mm. 81–94, present an opportunity for increased activity and dynamics in the instruments.

In the section from m. 89 to 94, the voice again speaks in rhythm, without pitch, as if overcome by emotion. The instruments go through the entire **RI**, using eighth-note triplets in modified sequence. Timpani, echoing the pitchless voice, rattle metallically. The downbeat of m. 94 is an elision, ending the **RI** (on F) and beginning the next sentence, which starts **RI** again (on B♭).

Mm. 94–98 provide our next small group. The vocal part commences the **RI**, and continues it uninterruptedly to the end of the sentence in m. 110. The singer slithers as he "spawns" and "crawls," in sequence. We use notes 1–6 in mm. 94–98 in the vocal line, but the instruments complete it in three measures (94–96), where the cello is merely a fawning echo of the singer.

The instruments, in m. 97, start the **I**-row, timpani sounding note 1, the flute, 2–5 with some repetitions; 6 and 7 are on the downbeat of m. 98, 8–10 in the timpani (mm. 98–99). Notes 11–12 serve also as 1–2 in the **RI** that begins in the cello, m. 99, and ends in the flute, m. 100. The horn, in mm. 100–101, reinforces the vocal line. Timpani, meanwhile, slowly terminate the old **I**-row, notes 8–12.

In m. 101, our *diabolus in musica* reappears, as the B♭ sounds with the climactic E in the voice. At the same time, the cello uses notes 2–8 of **RI**, continuing the flute rhythm of m. 100 in a more jagged line. (Note 1 is already in the flute and timpani.) To permit the *"rin-for-zan-do"* to ring out without competition, we markedly reduce the instrumental activity.

In mm. 103–104, the cello completes **RI**. Note 12 (F) is doubled in the timpani, who then move to F♯, not in continuation of the row but as preparation for and doubling of the vocal entry in m. 105.

The horn (m. 105) intones **I** 1–6, the cello has 7–9, the flute 10–12, a rare case of linear exhaustion of the row in a single measure.

The voice in mm. 105–110 has the second half of **RI**; considerable repetition makes possible the use of only six different "scale degrees" (pitch classes, if you prefer) in as many measures, in contrast to our procedure in m. 105 in the accompaniment. Timpani double the voice throughout.

The chords of mm. 106–107 were derived by using the **I**-row thus:

Fl.:	1	5	9
Hr.:	2	6	10
Vlc.:	3–4	7–8	11–12

M. 108 is limited to **RI** 1–6, in flute and cello. A quasi-sequence of these notes (**RI** 7–12) appears in the next measure. The cello part is "tailored" to end on F, not F♯, doubling the timpani and voice as the paragraph ends. This is a cadence of sorts, extended by the horn line, which restates the end of **RI** (6–12) in stentorian quarter-note triplets.

The six-measure interlude begins, in a way, in m. 111, but the overlap of voice and horn weakens that structural joint. More to the point is the "busy" canon after one measure, in which the *dux* in the flute uses **I**-row and the *comes* in the cello uses the **RI**. The rhythms are those of a regular canon, but the pitches of course are those of a canon in retrograde. The two wide leaps in mm. 113–114 suggest canon in inversion, to add to the (devilish?) ambiguity.

The canon ends, "suddenly," at m. 117.

Eighth step. The row usage for part three is worked out, tentatively: mm. 117–126, **IR**; 127–135, **RI+IR**; 136–149, **I+RI+IR**; 150–160, all except **O**; 161–173, **O** only. The vocal line will feature the newly added form as the increments are added; the instruments will use the remainder, except for the beginning and the end, where only a single row form appears.

Ninth step. We write the complete vocal part from m. 117 to the end.

Tenth step. We complete the accompaniment. The horn (mm. 117–121) is a coloristically modified doubling of the voice. The texture in these measures is somewhat heterophonic, as the instruments parallel the voice in rhythmic variation. **IR** (1–6) is in the voice, mm. 117–121. In the instruments, we see **IR** 1–6 in mm. 117–119; then—after some backtracking—**IR** 5–8 in mm. 120–122. Flute and cello engage in rhythmic imitation.

We continue the procedure of overlapping cells, following **IR** 5–8 (mm. 120–122) with 6–10 (mm. 123–125), the principle of which is similar to that of the use of common tones to relate adjacent chords.

Again, there is considerable doubling, and horn and cello engage in further tone painting. Flute and cello continue the imitation. A dotted rhythm in mm. 124–125 helps to relate timpani and voice parts.

We have saved the last notes of **IR** for the cadence in m. 126. Horn imitates cello, using **IR** 7–12.

RI (1–12) appears in the voice, mm. 128–132. It will sound familiar, since it is a transposition of **IR**.

Following the completion of **IR** (the last six notes) in m. 127, we begin a repetition of **IR**, hearing 1–6 in mm. 128–132. Thus, in these five measures, **RI** in the voice and **IR** in the accompaniment are treated contrapuntally.

In m. 128, **IR** skips from flute to cello. Repetition of **IR** 1–6 is heard in the cello in 129–131. In 131, **IR** 6 (C♯) enharmonically doubles **RI** 10 (D♭) in the voice. The texture thins out here, because excessive activity would work against comprehension of the words.

The horn in mm. 130–133 repeats **IR** 1–4, just heard in the cello, but in longer notes, to secure a degree of stability. The flute notes in m. 132 repeat **IR** 5–6, to balance the horn's repetition, and lead (as an anacrusis) to mm. 133–136, which are devoted almost exclusively to the rest of **IR** (7–12). The septuplets in the flute help suggest "swooping" and "swirling." Cello and timpani (mm. 133–134) repeat once more **IR** 1–6 (the timpani slides in tonal onomatopoeia), continuing with 7–12 in mm. 135–136. The voice, meanwhile, extends **RI** 10–12 by backtracking and repetition.

We use the overlap technique again in m. 134, where D♭-E♭-F serve both as the end of **RI** and as the beginning of the **I**-row.

From m. 134 to m. 141, the **I**-row (1–12) appears in the vocal part.

IR is completed in the instruments in m. 136. From m. 137 to m. 141, we use both **RI** (flute) and **IR** (cello); horn and timpani play subordinate roles.

We continue the rapid motion begun in the flute (m. 133) and also the repeated eighths used by voice and horn. The cello (m. 137) imitates the voice, then provides all of **IR** in a relatively independent line, but ends in parallel motion with the flute.

From m. 142 to m. 150, we plan to use **IR** in the voice, **I** and **RI** in the instruments. A pedal point F in the timpani provides an anchor. There is a partial canon between horn and cello (the pitch line is imitated, but not the rhythm).

Skipping back and forth between rows, the cello uses **RI** 1–6 in m. 142, **I** 1–6 in m. 143, **RI** 7–9 in m. 144, **I** 7–10 in m. 145, and completes both **RI** and **I** in m. 146. We undertook this somewhat "unorthodox" procedure partly to secure certain desired pitches, partly to gain increased surprise and tension to match the text.

In the flute, **I** (begun in m. 142) continues through m. 145, reaching a climax there on high B♭. **RI** follows (mm. 146–152) as the tensions ease somewhat. The horn uses **RI** from m. 141 to m. 147.

The "row texture" and the avoidance of simultaneous beginnings and endings of rows assists the creation of seamless continuity. On the other hand, there is general agreement in overall climax at m. 145. (The vocal climax will come later, in m. 155).

The "general cry" is accompanied by snarls in the horn, rough, dissonant chords in the cello.

There is a termination of rows in mm. 149–152: **IR** (in the voice), m. 150; **RI** (in the flute), m. 152; also (in the horn) in m. 149 (the note in 150 is just a doubling); **I** (in the cello), m. 151. From this point on, the style is more homophonic, the accompanimental parts in rather complete rhythmic agreement.

Accompanying the vocal line, which now seems more like 3/4 than 6/8 as it goes from **R** 1 to **R** 12 in mm. 150–154, the row is used in the following manner, to secure chords:

(mm. 151–152)
Fl.: **I** 1–6
Hr.: **RI** 1–6
Vlc.: **IR** 1–6

(mm. 153–154)
Fl.: **I** 7–12
Hr.: **RI** 7–12
Vlc.: **IR** 7–12

At m. 155, the vocal climax, on "hate" and "rage," the last notes are extended; the horn swoops up to high (written) C; the flute repeats its shrieking high B♭; while timpani thunder in minor sevenths, in support of the voice.

Except for the rhetorical question, the text ends in m. 157; but the vocal line starts a complete **O**-row in m. 156, creating a two-measure overlap. **O** 12 in m. 163 is C, suitably the dominant of F, since the remarks end with a question.

Homophony continues in the instruments, with rhythmic punctuation designed to create tension without covering up the text. From m. 156 to m. 162, all five row forms are in operation: **O** in the voice, **R** in the flute, **RI** in the horn, **IR** in the cello, and **I** in the timpani. The rows unfold simultaneously—for example, in m. 159, one hears notes 6 and 7 of the several row forms.

The staccato chords provide a rhythmic strength and consensus that reinforces the meaning of the words.

The rather rare use of the timpani for a melodic line is possible due to the prevalence of stepwise motion in the row itself. It will take a skilled performer to do it well, nevertheless.

The procedure for securing chords used in mm. 156 162 is a somewhat aleatoric one, since the element of chance enters into the determination of what notes sound simultaneously. However, as in all nonfunctional harmony, linear considerations compensate for apparent lack of orthodox sonorities and relationships, and in fact help to explain them.

Following the completion of the vocal part in m. 163, we now must decide what to do in the coda. We plan a brief cadential extension, by prolonging the last notes in the horn and cello and repeating the last notes of the vocal phrase. The latter are shared by all four instruments, as the phrase is fragmented. With this final "dismemberment"—again justified by the text—we now face the last seven measures of music.

The somewhat modified use of introduction materials for the closing measures of the coda seems thoroughly appropriate. Beginning and ending on F, our "tonic," we provide the "frame" for the "picture," and suggest the moral that commonly was addressed to the audience in Beaumarchais's time. There is a similar rhetorical effect in Richard Strauss's tone-poem *Till Eulenspiegel* and Weber's *Invitation to the Dance,* though some misguided conductors of Berlioz's eloquent orchestration of the latter work actually omit the closing part of the frame!

Comparison with the introduction will reveal the few alterations. Timpani are allowed time to retune. The prominence of C and E and the absence of F in the measures preceding 173 make the appearance of that note all the more necessary and conclusive.

Eleventh step. We carefully check the score for errors. We pay particular attention to changing dynamic levels, changes from arco to pizzicato and vice versa, missing accidentals (which happens very easily in a chromatic style), ease and facility of performance (especially in the fingerings of the intervals and chords in the cello), and so forth. We do this twice, once going measure-by-measure through the entire score, a second time following *each part* through. The vocal part should be sung, as technique and range permit, to see if alterations are needed. In our own review of the work, we observed that the tempo of part three seemed too fast for proper "delivery" of its contents. We therefore added, after the work was finished, the *poco meno mosso* (see m. 117) and the further slight reduction at m. 161 for the final vocal phrase, the instruments to follow the voice (*colla parte*), with resumption of *a tempo* (the preceding tempo) for the coda.

Twelfth step. We copy the parts in preparation for the performance, inserting rhythmic cues where needed, in small notes. We are sure to put any horn cues in concert pitch (actual sound). Cues written in the horn part may be transposed up a fifth to allow the horn player to relate them to what he or she is called upon to play. Measure numbers are marked, every five or ten measures or at the beginning of each staff line. We are careful to plan ahead to avoid awkward page turns. It might be well, for the first few rehearsals at least, to have a conductor (who should have a copy of the full score).

We are now ready to tackle our second medium-length composition. Like the previous example, it will have a text by Beaumarchais, but one with quite a different structure and style. We plan to use SATB chorus, in which there may be solo-voice parts—but no special soloists are called for. The character of the poem suggests the use of a lute, guitar, or harp. This will provide a sense of antiquity that is not altogether out of place—though the music written for it need not sound antique! The limited means of accompaniment will permit the text and the voices to emerge without having to compete with it. The instrument should create mood and provide pitch support for the chorus.

The text is from Act 2 of *The Marriage of Figaro.* The son is sung by Chérubin (cherubino) a page boy about to leave for military service, the Countess, on whom he has a youthful "crush," while Suzanne (Figaro's fiancée) accompanies him with the Countess's guitar. The two ladies listen in mock seriousness to his melancholy ditty, which Beaumarchais refers to as a ballad. Indeed, the style and form suggest one of the old medieval secular monophonic types. There is a refrain in the second line of each stanza, suggesting the medieval *rondeau* rather than the *ballade.*[6]

My steed was weary and slow
  (Alas, but my heart is in pain)
Our heads alike hanging low
As we wandered over the plain.

As we wandered over the plain
  (Alas, but my heart is in pain)
My tears I strove to restrain
As I rode with a loose-hanging rein.

6. See *KMF*, page 217.

As I rode with a loose-hanging rein
  (Alas, but my heart is in pain)
The Queen passing by said, "Pray tell me why
You ride with a tear in your eye."

Why you ride with a tear in your eye
  (Alas, but my heart is in pain)
I shall ne'er see my true love again.
I shall ne'er see my true love again.[7]

Beaumarchais, in the first printed edition (1785), describes Chérubin as "diffident," a "charming young scamp" filled with "an undefined and restless desire," "entering adolescence . . . with no understanding of what is happening to him."[8]

A note in the English edition[9] indicates that the words are to be sung to the tune "*Marlbrough s'en va t'en Guerre,*" a popular song of Beaumarchais's day, clearly calling for solo voice and guitar in any stage performance. However, we are extracting the text for our own purposes and (as often happens in choral song) permit the group to express collectively the personal feelings of the individual members. The refrain, always in parentheses, we plan to allot to a solo voice (each time to a *different* part of the SATB chorus), the other lines are to be sung by the whole ensemble. For the repetition in line 16, we may use a solo voice (perhaps the four soli, *a quattro*) as a final sad echo of line 15.

Close inspection of the poem reveals a fascinatingly intricate structure that belies its surface simplicity. Each stanza has a different rhyme pattern. The scheme for the four stanzas is *abab bbbb bbcc cbbb.* In the sixteen lines, there are only three homophones. Eleven of the lines end with *-ain* (or *-ein*), three with *why* (or *eye*), and two with *-ow* (*slow* or *low*).

In addition, the fourth lines of stanzas 1, 2, and 3 are repeated as the first lines of the immediately following stanzas. Further line repetition at the very end of the poem recalls the practice of extension by repetition that we have observed in musical examples, including Example 13.1.

If we designate *R* as the refrain and use lower-case letters to indicate new (or repeated) text, the following form emerges: *aRbc cRde eRfg gRhh.* If we omit *R,* an interpolation, we have: *abc cde efg ghh.* Here we see backtracking such as that employed in our serial technique in Example 13.1. It is most instructive to see repetition, interpolation, backtracking, and so forth, in a medium other than music. It is a further demonstration of our view that many of the fundamental principles of music are common to all the arts.[10]

The poem is clearly in triple meter. The number of feet per line (in music, the number of measures per phrase) seems at first to be three. But the eleventh line will not fit, so the solution obviously is to have four-foot lines, to be treated in the following manner:

7. From Act 2, *The Marriage of Figaro,* by Caron de Beaumarchais, translated by John Wood, Penguin Books, (1964, reprinted 1976). Copyright © 1964, John Wood. Used with permission.
8. *Ibid.*, page 222.
9. Page 134.
10. See *KMF,* Chapter 1.

A diagram of the poem, similar to diagrams we designed in *KMF,* reveals the several hierarchical levels and overlapping structural units.

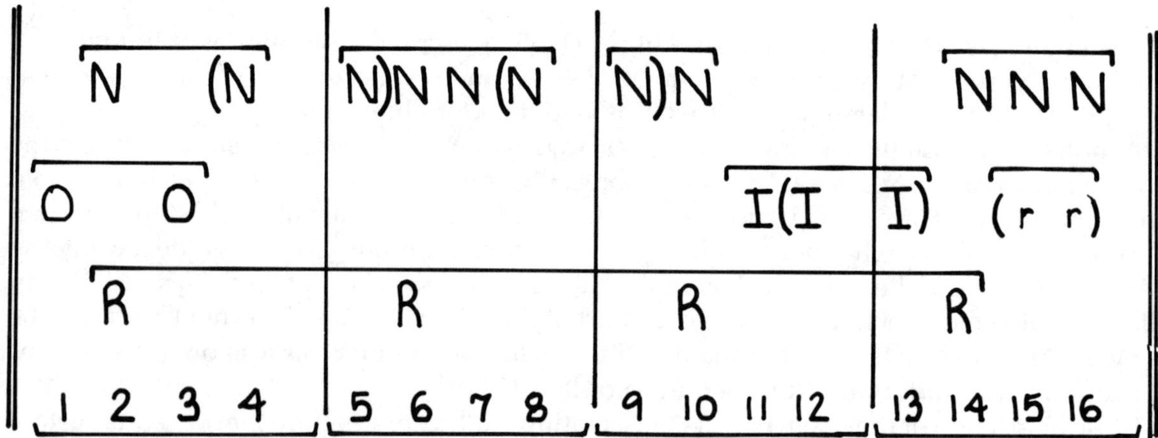

Key: Numbers indicate line numbers.
N indicates the *-ain/-ein* rhyme.
O indicates the *-ow* rhyme.
I indicates the *why/eye* rhyme.
r indicates the terminal repetition.
R indicates the refrain.
Brackets below numbers show the four stanzas.
Parentheses ( ) show line repetitions.

At this point, we must give the translator due recognition. Clearly, he had a most difficult task in balancing the two demands of poetic form and literary content, two taskmasters driving the translator in what at times must have seemed to be incompatible directions.

To facilitate comparison with the original, we append it here. Entitled "Romance," it has eight (not four) stanzas, or "couplets." The "true love" (*la marraine*) is the singer's godmother. The Queen offers to serve in the same capacity, and as inducement promises a captain's daughter as future bride, but the persistent lover declines, preferring death to consolation.

1er couplet
Mon coursier hors d'haleine,
(Que mon coeur, mon coeur a de peine!)
J'errais de plaine en plaine,
Au gré du destrier.

2e couplet

Au gré du destrier,
Sans varlet, n'écuyer,
§ *Là près d'une fontaine,*
(Que mon coeur, mon coeur a de peine!)
Songeant à ma marraine,
Sentais mes pleurs couler.

3e couplet

Sentais mes pleurs couler,
Prêt à me désoler;
Je gravais sur un frêne,
(Que mon coeur, mon coeur a de peine!)
Sa lettre sans la mienne;
Le roi vint à passer.

4e couplet

Le roi vint à passer,
Ses barons, son clergier.
______*Beau page, dit la reine,*
(Que mon coeur, mon coeur a de peine!)
Qui vous met à la gêne?
Qui vous fait tant plorer?

5e couplet

Qui vous fait tant plorer?
Nous faut le déclarer.
______*Madame et Souveraine,*
(Que mon coeur, mon coeur a de peine!)
J'avais une marraine,
Que toujours adorai.§§

6e couplet

Que toujours adorai:
Je sens que j'en mourrai.
______*Beau page, dit la reine,*
(Que mon coeur, mon coeur a de peine!)
N'est-il qu'une marraine?
Je vous enservirai.

7e couplet

Je vous en servirai;
Mon page vous ferai;

§In performance, one begins with this line (Beaumarchais's note).
§§Here the Countess stops the pageboy. The balance is not sung in performance (B's note). From Beaumarchais, *Theatre,* ed. Garnier-Flammarion, Paris, © 1965.

Puis à ma jeune Hélène,
(Que mon coeur, mon coeur a de peine!)
Fille d'un capitaine,
Un jour vous marîrai.

8e couplet
Un jour vous marîrai.
——*Nenni, n'en faut parler;*
Je veux, traînent ma chaîne,
(Que mon coeur, mon coeur a de peine!)
Mourir de cette peine,
Mais non m'en consoler.

We have completed most of our precompositional tasks. A slightly modified strophic form seems to be the most appropriate design for the music that is to adorn our chosen words. Although a story is told, there is no change of mood, no growth or increase in intensity, no dramatic climax such as we observed in Example 13.1.

A chromatic style might be out of place here. One could well consider a pandiatonic style, perhaps using an artificial, perhaps a pentatonic, scale. The melancholy mood need not call for minor mode—many of Schubert's and Mahler's most poignant utterances convey their message by the very fact that even a bright major mode is unable to alleviate the pain of grief or loss—it is a type of irony, very subtle, but apparent to the receptive ear.

In pursuance of this thought, we decide to use the Lydian mode. It is even brighter than major, since the fourth scale degree is raised. (Perhaps this is why Beethoven used it for his Prayer of Thanksgiving in his *String Quartet,* Op. 132, third movement.)

An introduction, interludes between stanzas, and a coda will enlarge the form. The accompanying instrument will be a harp, whose basically diatonic construction is admirably suited to our chosen mode. Its tone, as a plucked stringed instrument, resembles that of the guitar, but its greater sonority is a better balance for the chorus than the smaller instrument, which is ideal as accompaniment to the solo voice.

We will not use any motives to speak of. There is plenty of repetition as it is, and the text has enough structure to support even an amorphous musical adornment. The pensive character throughout suggests that we use mostly descending lines, without allowing that determination to be unduly restrictive.

We may now take our first steps "over the plain" of the manuscript paper, our pace "slow" but (let us hope) without heads "hanging low."

Example 13.2 *Composing a medium-length work for SATB chorus and harp, based upon the ballade "My Steed Was Weary and Slow," from* The Marriage of Figaro, *by Beaumarchais.*

First step. We tentatively decide on overall length, then the length of the introduction in the solo harp. The tempo, obviously, should be slow. Allowing for some asymmetry to break what would be rather intolerable symmetry (four times 4+4+4+4), we come up with the following: 7+22+7+22+7+22+7+22+7. This asymmetrical repetition allows for seven-measure instrumental passages surrounding the twenty-two-measure stanzas. The stanzas, in turn, are composed of another asymmetrical arrangement: 5+6+5+6. The first six is designed to allow a bit of languor (not too much, please!) for the sad refrain; the second six is to permit a bit of extension appropriate to a cadence, and to balance line 2.

Second step. Following the drawing of bar lines of the introduction and stanza 1, we compose the music for the harp in mm. 1–8. We write pandiatonically in C Lydian mode, using a signature in the harp part only. In the voices, F♯ is used as an accidental to help make clear the tonal center, C. Harmony is largely but not exclusively quartal. There is a cadence in m. 8.

[STANZA 1]
5
mf
My
dim.
p
steed was wea-ry and slow
p subito
pp
9
(non dim.)
sempre arp.
non arp.

Third step. We write the text underlay of stanza 1 below the vocal staves, consistent with our predeterminations, but allowing for occasional expansion or extension. Then we compose the music for mm. 8–12 in the following order: 1) soprano line; 2) bass line in the harp accompaniment; 3) the balance of the accompaniment above the bass line; 4) the ATB lines so as to be consistent with the accompaniment, using common tones and stepwise motion where possible. We write homophonically, the text in rhythmic unison, but we attempt linear activity consistent with that style.

The chorus begins on an "open" fifth, to suggest antiquity. The end of line 1, at m. 11, uses VI rather than I or V, to avoid a sense of harmonic cadence.

Fourth step. Write the text underlay of lines 2, 3, and 4. For line 2 we plan to use a solo tenor voice.

We "stretch" line 2 by repeating "alas" and by allowing a brief pause prior to the text that follows. The brief separation between "pain" and "our" is balanced by suppression of the expected pause between lines 3 and 4.

In line 4 we again use "backtracking," as a complement to the continuous motion in m. 24, repeating the words "as we wandered." We have noted several times before that such repetition is a familiar and useful "signal" to the listener in pre- and postcadential extensions.

This brings us to m. 29. We now return to m. 12 in order to continue the bass line.

Fifth step. We write the music for the tenor solo, starting on E, the last soprano note on line 1. The line begins with descending broken chords, then ascends stepwise to C. This is the tonic, but we harmonize it with a dissonant chord in the harp in order to accentuate the word "pain." The texture is polyphonic in the accompaniment for a few measures, then is largely homophonic. The notes in the harp's melody line (mm. 10–16) are formed by a descending stepwise line with displaced octaves. In mm. 13–15, one detects a brief canon at the octave after two beats.

Consonant triads in m. 17 prepare us for the dissonant chord in m. 18. This is inverted in m. 19. Because it continues as the harmony for the next word, it serves as a link between the lines. Harmonics and reduced dynamics in m. 19 heighten overall expressivity.

Sixth step. With no separation between lines 3 and 4 of the text, we decide to set both lines in a single step. First we set the complete soprano line, with mostly stepwise motion in an arch-shaped curve. This ends in m. 29 on a note that may be harmonized later by C:I. Then we compose the accompaniment, bass line first. The other vocal lines are written last. These are consistent with the harmonies in the accompaniment, and provide occasional melismas and contrasting rhythms.

Triplet sixteenths (m. 25) and open-spaced chords (m. 28) prior to the cadence in m. 29 provide intensity, contrast, and variety.

We designed our cadential harmonies to "work" without sounding familiar or platitudinous. If the root progression here is unorthodox, at least the lines are clear and direct, as they should be in all non-functional harmony. The Lydian mode provides additional reason for providing the unusual.

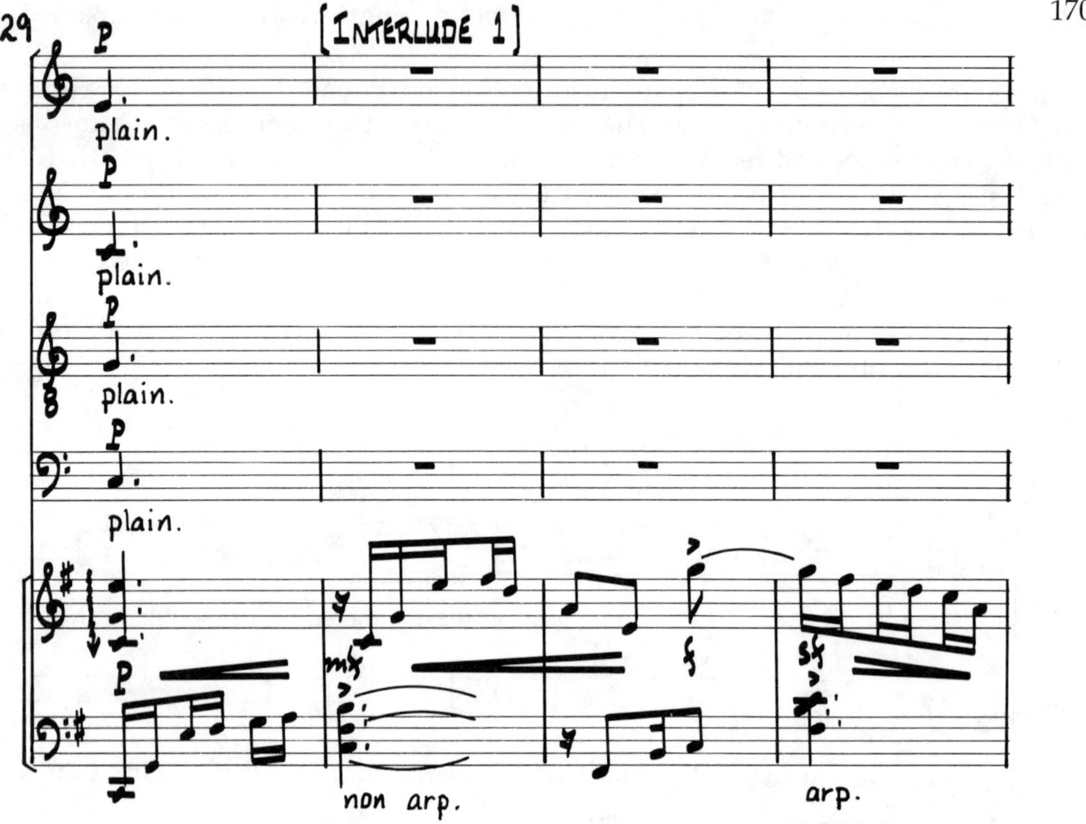

Seventh step. We write the first of our three interludes, all of which are essentially repetitions of the introduction. This procedure is common practice in strophic form—see, for example, Schubert's song "Who Is Sylvia." We write, taking particular care of the connections at both ends of interlude 1.

We make a few small alterations in the opening measures of interlude 1, to maintain a higher level of momentum than was needed in the introduction. The change in m. 34 is designed to keep the sixteenths in the lower register, to permit the upper-line melody to emerge more clearly.

Eighth step. We now compose stanza 2. Except for the double anacrusis (♩♩|♩), it begins with stanza 1. We write the text of line 1 under the four vocal staves. Then we write the music for these words, using material from line 1 of stanza 1, not line 4, though we hear the words of the latter line.

41
Solo (BACKSTAGE OR BEHIND THE AUDIENCE)
(A - las, a - las,
P Sub.
P Sub.
45
but my heart is in pain)
non arp.
sfz
sfz
P Sub.

After wavering between alternatives, respecting the vocal setting of line 2, we decide that we cannot treat male and female voices equally—since it is the lover who pines for his lass—nor can we omit the female voices, because that would upset the balance we had in mind. A third possibility comes as sudden revelation, reflecting the truth of the cliché about necessity being the mother of invention: why not use the female voices in alternation with the male, but backstage or behind the audience, to suggest the distant beloved? That adds a slightly theatrical touch, but in this instance a thoroughly justifiable one.

The harp part is modified slightly, the reduction in dynamics helping to ensure the audibility of the voice. Line 2 is written, then, for solo soprano.

Line 3 poses an interesting problem. Unlike the other third lines, there are here only *three* stressed syllables—the comparable lines have *four.* We consider and then reject "My *tears* I *strove to* re-*strain*" because of the awkward accent on the word "to." The alternate solution, to prolong the last stressed syllable, seems preferable. As a happy result, there is a melismatic treatment of *strain* in the word "restrain," which accords with the sense of the words.

M. 54 is an alteration of 25. We have one syllable here instead of two. Our text suggests greater tension and activity, hence the thirty-second-notes in the harp. Played as a glissando, they are, however, less distinct than if individually fingered.

57
[INTERLUDE 2]
P
loose-hang-ing rein.
P
loose-hang-ing rein.
P
loose-hang-ing rein.
P
loose-hang-ing rein.
(P)
(non-cresc.)
non arp.
61

In mm. 55–56, the chords are broken in descending motion, as a symbol of the "loose-hanging rein." Changes in texture, but without alteration of the harmonic structure, continue to the cadence in m. 58.

Ninth step. In interlude 2, we continue texture variation. Dynamics remain *piano,* "loose-hanging," in contrast to interlude 1, where dynamic changes were consistent with the "wandering" described in the poem.

Tenth step. Before composing the music for stanza 3, we prepare the text underlay. Music to fit the words follows. Finally, we write the accompaniment.

It is quite proper—indeed, statistically normal—for the stanzas to be exact replicas of each other, with alterations of the type utilized in stanza 2 taken for granted. However, having begun the use of textual variation in the accompaniment, we decide that it would be best to continue it. These additional changes in stanza 3 are quite evident in the chordal setting of line 1, but the texture is linear in the accompaniment for line 2, so that this type of variation is not appropriate here. The bass solo has his turn with the "alas" interpolation.

73
mf
f
las, but my heart is in pain)
non arp.
sfz
sfz
77
mf
The Queen pass-ing by said,
mf
The Queen pass-ing by said,
mf
The Queen pass-ing by said,
Tutti
mf
The Queen pass-ing by said,
p
mf

We should mention that we planned the solo interpolations so that they need not be transposed except for the octave. However, some contraltos may find the opening note (E) a bit high, and the choral director may wish to assign that entry to a mezzo.

Again, a small texture change (in m. 75).

Line 3, which has the greatest number of syllables of any line in the poem, must be handled with care. In m. 80, the text rhythm could be either ♩♪ or ♪♩; we have selected the latter in order to gain desired separation prior to the quotation of the Queen's words.

Another oddity here is that although line 3 ends on the word "why," which is important to the rhyme scheme, our music runs on to the word "ride," which gains considerable emphasis as a result. Also, the backtracking to the word "why" very appropriately anticipates (and even helps to make logical!) the repetition of "why" in line 1 of stanza 4. The accompaniment texture here parallels that of stanza 1.

Postcadential motion in m. 87 leads us to the next section.
Eleventh step. We now can easily write the notes for interlude 3.

89
(non arp.)
93
[STANZA 4]
Why you ride with a
Why you ride with a
Why you ride with a
Why you ride with a
P sub.

As stanza 3 was parallel to stanza 1, after the variations of stanza 2, so interlude 3 is closer to interlude 1 than was interlude 2. The alterations in mm. 89–93 are almost unnoticeable. The triplet sixteenths in m. 92 were suggested by their appearance in m. 91. In that measure, the number of notes (more than used heretofore in the corresponding place) creates a magnitude of sonority not previously attained. It was suggested as a way of dealing, in the accompaniment, with the inner feelings of the rider-poet, as he tries to control himself in the wake of the Queen's request for an explanation.

Interlude 3 ends and stanza 4 begins in m. 95.

Twelfth step. We compose stanza 4. As we mentioned earlier, the first line of this stanza is irregular in its repetition of line 4 of the preceding stanza, in that it includes, also, the last word of line 3! As a result, we have a double anacrusis in line 1.

The accompaniment continues its repetition, with slightly varied texture.

It is the turn of the alto to sing the interpolation. If the first note is too high, it may be sung in the alternative manner suggested by the *ossia*. This singer, like the soprano solo, should be at some distance from the ensemble and the audience.

105
mf
I shall ne'er see my
f
Tutti
mf
pain
I shall ne'er see my
I shall ne'er see my
I shall ne'er see my
non arp.
sfz
sfz
p sub.
mf
109
cresc.
dim.
mf
POCO MENO MOSSO
Solo
true love a - gain
I shall ne'er see
cresc.
dim.
mf
Solo
true love a - gain
I shall ne'er see
cresc.
dim.
mf
solo
true love a - gain
I shall ne'er see
cresc.
dim.
mf
Solo
true love a - gain
I shall ne-ver see
POCO MENO MOSSO
cresc.

The variation idea spreads like an infection! In mm. 111–112, where the fourth and last line is begun, we hear solo voices only, not the full chorus; and to heighten the effect of these voices coming from a distance, the harp does not play at all. Further, there is a slight moderation in the tempo. The soprano and tenor sing "ne'er," having but one pitch, but the basses, having two pitches, sing "ne-ver." The alto setting is designed to use an appoggiatura.

In m. 113, where our text backtracks in order to make the line complete, the full chorus re-enters and the previous tempo is resumed. Variation in the harp part provides a wispy, descending line that mirrors the singer's mood. A brief surge of harmonic energy provides the cadence in mm. 115–116.

Thirteenth step. We originally planned for the introduction to serve also as coda. But now that we have arrived at the point where the coda should begin, it seems more in keeping with the text to allow the music to die out. There is measure-for-measure correspondence, but considerable thinning and some compression. The latter permits us to end on the downbeat of m. 123, as planned. Reduced tempos and fermatas assist the morendo.

We should make a few observations at this time. First, the apparently "easy" strophic form poses unexpected problems and opportunities—it does not just follow automatically from the first stanza. Second, our completed work *is* primarily in strophic form, but we have allowed it to take on some aspects of variation form as well. Third, the form of the text and that of the music provide a kind of *counterpoint of forms.* We analyzed the structure of the poem earlier, and noted that no two stanzas had the same rhyme scheme—an important element in the form, in striking contrast to the music, whose four lines per stanza are always the same (they could be indicated as *abcd,* four times). Text repetition in line 1 of stanzas 2–4 is not reflected in the music, except for some similarity in the soprano part.

We check the score for accuracy and prepare parts, though in the present instance they need not be extracted, since the chorus will require full score. Multiple copies, then, are needed for all concerned.

Exercise 13.1 *Write a medium-length work taking either Example 13.1 or 13.2 as a model for form and procedure. An essay descriptive of your thought processes and creative intentions should accompany each of the several steps. Ideally, each step should be approved before the next one is attempted.*

Exercise 13.2 *Write a medium-length work using one of the other forms mentioned in paragraph 2, page 129. Prepare a diagram or outline of your intentions and have it approved before you begin. Accompany your work with a descriptive essay.*

14. Composing a Large-Scale Instrumental Work

It is evident, considering the length of Chapter 13, that we must be content here to compose a single example. To do more would tax the reader's patience, not to mention the publisher's faith in the author's sense of the realistic.

Besides, our methodology and approach should be well established, if not altogether predictable, by now. The enormous range of structural possibilities in the area of extended compositions is suggested by the author in *KMF*, particularly chapter 21 (rondo forms), 22 (altered rondo forms), 23 (sonata form), 24 (near-sonata forms), and 26 (works comprising several movements). Review of the illustrations and diagrams in those chapters and examination of the literature suggested by the exercises at the close of those chapters will prepare the reader for the compositional activities in this, our last chapter.

It may be observed that we are not primarily concerned with the musical language or style that is employed. It would be futile to attempt to bring the reader up to the brink of the chasm that marks the end of the past and the beginning of the future of music. The razor's edge of the avant-garde may at times cut through the brush in order to reveal more clearly the road to the future; at other times, it may simply tumble into the abyss and disappear from view. Reports of the demise of the avant-garde, like the announcements of the death of God, are not necessarily to be taken at face value; but those who make these pronouncements bear watching, if only because they reveal symptoms the underlying causes of which reside elsewhere—a phenomenon well known to the medical profession. The best way to discover the latest trends is to study published scores of composers who are attracting attention by the novelty of their style. Some of the new trends will undoubtedly be incorporated in the language of music, others will be discarded, as the culling and sifting process continues its historic, inexorable march.

Accordingly, we have decided to attempt a work of sizable proportions and complexity in a medium not hitherto explored by the author. Continuing our evident fondness for altering or combining known forms rather than inventing new ones, we decide to write a work that has elements of sonata form, rondo, variation, and the concerto, for a medium that has been little utilized until recently—percussion ensemble.

With two string quartets and a quartet for piano and strings behind us, we think it is time to compose a percussion quartet—that is to say, a work for four percussionists, each of whom has several instruments at hand. Notation for percussion is still evolving and is in as chaotic a state as that for the widely performed lute in the fifteenth and sixteenth centuries.[1] The need for literature is enormous, with good performers and ensembles appearing in ever-greater numbers. Many students now learning their craft by necessity have to play many transcriptions.

After discarding several sketches, we finally came to a fairly detailed and comprehensive set of particulars, which we now outline.

Table 14.1 *Precompositional considerations for an extended work for percussion ensemble.*

FORM	Sonata form (slow introduction, exposition, development, recapitulation, coda). Exposition and recapitulation to combine elements of the concerto and of rondo form.
MEDIUM	Percussion ensemble: a quartet of percussionists (I, II, III, IV), each performer to have a variety of instruments.
STYLE	The music is largely of unpitched sounds. We explore asymmetrical rhythms and meters, using as our basic time signature 19/16, in which the 19 is 6+6+7, further subdivided (2+2+2)+(3+3)+(2+2+3).
MOTIVES	The exposition, with rondo structure having *a, b, c, d,* and *e* sections, will have a variety of motives—to be worked out later. These will be *combined*, in the development, and some of them *varied* in the recapitulation.
LENGTH, TEMPO	Introduction (slow), 27 mm. (11+9+7); exposition, 60 mm. (8+9+7+8+6+7+5+6+4); development, 40 mm. (10+9+8+7+6); recapitulation, 51 mm. (8+9+8+7+7+6+6); coda, 27 mm., balancing the introduction in mm. but not in performing time (10+9+8). Tempo: ♪ = 180, with the 16th-note constant in value.
MOOD, CHARACTER	Introduction: vague, impressionistic, somewhat aleatoric. Otherwise, rather tense, nervous, energetic, positive. Rondo form will require adjustments and short departures from overall mood.
DYNAMICS, CLIMAX	Main climax, end of development. Secondary climax, in the coda.
AUDIENCE	Concert. Might be useful as score for modern dance company.

1. See Willi Apel, *The Notation of Polyphonic Music 900–1600*, The Mediaeval Academy of America, 1942, Part 1, Chapter 4.

A few additional comments are in order. The exposition subdivisions—listed under "length" and implied under "motives" in connection with the rondo form we plan to use—are as follows:

Length/Measures:	8	9	7	8	6	7	5	6	4
Rondo element:	a^1	b	a^2	c	a^3	d	a^4	e	a^5
Meter:	$\frac{19}{16}$	C	$\frac{19}{16}$	$\frac{7}{8}$	$\frac{19}{16}$	$\frac{3}{4}$	$\frac{19}{16}$	$\frac{9}{8}$	$\frac{19}{16}$

The a-sections grow progressively shorter (8, 7, 6, 5, 4); the contrasting sections exhibit a similar progression (9, 8, 7, 6). All a-sections are in 19/16 meter, the others are, respectively, in C, 7/8, 3/4, and 9/8. The sixteenths per measure in parts b, c, and d number 16, 14, and 12, respectively, which means that these contrasting sections have not only fewer measures, but shorter ones as well. The measures in e are only one sixteenth-note shorter than those in a.

The development has five subdivisions. With the meter to be determined later, the plan otherwise is:

Length/Measures:	10	9	8	7	6
Motivic elements:	$(b+c)$	$(d+e)$	$(c+d)$	$(b+e+d)$	$(b+c+d+e)$

Here the progression forms a straight line rather than a wavy one. The a-elements, already considerably exposed, are not used. The others appear in various combinations of increasing complexity, leading to the climax near the end.

Our recapitulation is shorter than the exposition by nine measures, a result of our plan to omit two a-parts. (As just indicated, a has been well exposed already.) The a-parts, when they do appear, are variations rather than restatements, in contrast to the succession of a-parts in the exposition, which were unvaried except in length. The b-, c-, d-, and e-parts are exact restatements.

Length/Measures:	8	9	8	7	7	6	6
Rondo element:	a^{v^1}	b	c	a^{v^2}	d	e	a^{v^3}

Superscripts (a^{v^1}, etc.) refer to the variations, of which there are three.

Finally, the coda. It is a brief second development section. Its twenty-seven measures, unlike those of the introduction (which are 11+9+7, subdivided 6+5, 5+4, 4+3) are 10+9+8, and we will attempt to avoid subdivision if this is possible.

Length/Measures:	10	9	8
Rondo element:	$(b+d)$	$(c+e)$	(a^{v^4})

The first two subdivisions use combinations not found in the development section, and a (which did not appear at all in the development, and which had two unexpected disappearances in the recapitulation) makes a counterbalancing appearance in a fourth variation, which is of the same length as the first a in the exposition—one of those nice mirroring frames again. The meters will correspond to those used earlier, and thus are not indicated.

How does all of this elaborate structure tie in with the concerto, one might ask? We have decided that the a-sections, and these *only*, are to be tutti and *forte* (*f* or *ff*). The others are to be solos, duos, or trios, and largely soft (*pp*, *p*, or *mf*) with the exception of the end of the development, where we have $b+c+d+e$ played by four players.

As *a* is the tutti in our quasi-concerto, so *b* is associated with percussionist I, *c* with II, *d* with III, and *e* with IV. When the "solo" player holds forth, the others may serve as light background. Everyone thus has an opportunity to be soloist and part of the accompaniment, too, as in standard jazz-band practice.

Disposition of the percussion instruments among the four performers is indicated below. First and third have instruments without defined pitches, each instrument allotted to a specific space on the staff. No clef is used. Second and fourth performers play instruments with precise pitches, II using treble clef for the prevailingly high notes, IV bass clef for the timpani. Following standard practice, the xylophone, glockenspiel, and celesta are written an octave lower than they sound; we use a treble clef with an "8" above it to indicate that the music sounds an octave higher.

From time to time, we shall employ serial procedures, but this practice is only intermittent and not constant. We have chosen the following notes for our row.

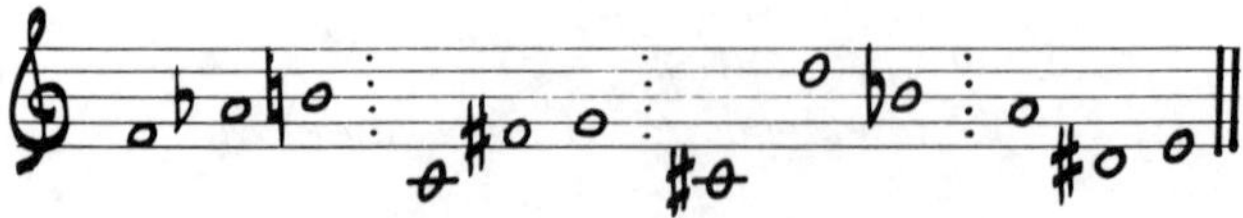

The largest number of intervals are dissonances: five minor seconds and three tritones. There are two minor thirds, one major third, and no perfect fourths or fifths. If we add the interval between 12 and 1, there is a sixth minor second.

The three-note cells create a diminished triad, F-A♭-B; a quasi-quartal harmony, G-C-F♯, a major-minor third, B♭-C♯-D (heard as B♭-D♭-D♮), and another quasi-quartal chord, E-A-D♯. None of these is likely to suggest any tonal center, but the many half-steps will help provide close voice-leading connections between these cells, if we decide to use them harmonically.

There may be those who feel that all of this is too highly structured, too highly planned, too intellectual, too mathematical, too cold-blooded. The response to that charge is that what we have done is composition; to compose is to put things together. We have created a blueprint for our tonal house, as an architect creates one for a house of brick, mortar, stone, glass, and cement. And one must remember that, like the architect, we may always alter our plans if they appear to need alteration. To compose otherwise is to improvise without a conception, and that is foreign to art as well as to nature. Details may be improvised, but the conceived musical cell—with its array of parameters that resemble genetic structure in a fertilized egg—is necessary as a shaping power that precedes gestation and continues until birth, which is to say the completed work.

But it is time we began our project.

Example 14.1 *Composing an extended work for percussion quartet, one movement in modified sonata form.*

First step. We commence with part one of the introduction, which is eleven measures subdivided 6+5. We will attempt to introduce most of the instruments, gradually, in a setting that suggests that a large form is about to unfold. To accomplish the latter, we begin with sustained tremolos, *ppp,* in timpani and suspended cymbal. Percussion II and III play *ad libitum,* unfettered by meter or bar line, in a brief dialog, in mm. 1–6. In mm. 7–11, the roles are reversed; unmeasured notes in timpani and temple blocks are heard against bass drum and celesta. The row, 1–12, moves from xylophone to timpani to celesta in a zigzag course. The glockenspiel echoes the last two notes in augmentation.

Introduction

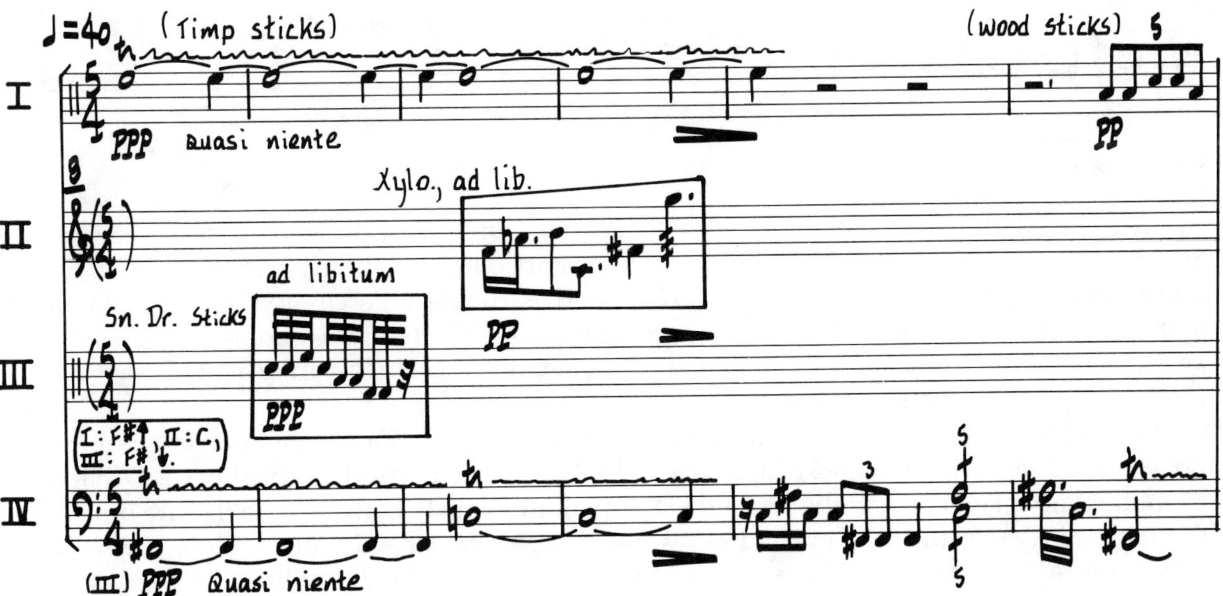

Second step. Part two of the introduction is nine measures, 5+4. In view of the somewhat amorphous character and improvisatory style of part one, we attempt, in the interest of unity, to relate part two to part one. Mm. 12–16 derive from 1–6. Percussion II part is related to the earlier tritone tremolos on F♯ and C in percussion IV. The timpani (percussion IV) play a varied echo of the *ad libitum* xylophone part (the row, notes 1–6). The unmeasured parts are now in I and III instead of II and III.

The next four measures (17–20) are similarly related to 7–11. Part I is an inversion of the notes played earlier by III. Glockenspiel and xylophone (in II) derive their pitches C♯-D-B♭-A from the timpani (in IV), and the repeated D♯ and E, previously in the celesta (II), are now in the timpani (IV). With these pitched notes, we complete a second "tour" of the row.

For contrast, we abandon the measured procedure in mm. 17–20, return to a mixture of measured and unmeasured music in mm. 21–24, and again use only measured rhythm in mm. 25–27. These few moments of general agreement provide opportunities for the conductor or leader of the group to ensure the limited nature of the aleatory procedures. In our notation, we have drawn bar lines across the entire four-staff system to indicate the requirement for agreement on the downbeat that follows.

The dynamic level in part two is higher than it was in part one, which was between *ppp* and *mf*. The latter part of this section (mm. 17–20) includes a dynamic range that goes from *p* to *fff*, with each line pursuing a relatively independent course. The *piano* tremolos continue the previously established tone quality and level, while the threatening but unconsummated crescendos that lead nowhere are foreshadowings of things to come.

Third step. Completing the introduction, with the third part, seven measures, 4+3, we enlarge our measures in advance, to allow for more notes as we build up to a climax.

The chief unifying elements here are to be found in III, where bass drum and tom-toms play a zigzag ascending line three times, with ever-increasing repetition of the last note. Although it is in measured rhythm, the changes from septuplet through quadruplet to half-note triplet give the impression of free improvisation and increasing urgency as the dynamic level rises from *p* to *ff*. The tremolo on the suspended cymbal in I provides a parallel crescendo in support of III.

Meanwhile, II and IV seem to have gone quite mad. The xylophone, between m. 21 and m. 25, has all twelve tones, but not in row order; once it reaches the climactic tritone, derived from the opening measures in the timpani (mm. 1–6), it simply repeats it as though in a state of frozen fury. Timpani, in IV, are busy providing their own rhythmic version of the progression sounded by the xylophone, in a quasi-stretto in augmentation, in two groups: the first (unmeasured) in the three boxed groups, from *f* to *ff*, the second (measured tremolos) rising from *p* to *ff*.

The general idea here was to provide a rather controlled and planned chaos, in preparation for the more orderly procedures that we hope to establish in the ensuing exposition. There should be a clean and precise termination of sounds at the end of m. 27; the fermata indicates our desire to have a separation before the exposition begins. There should be no relaxation of tension for listeners at this point; rather, they should sense suspended animation. Too many things have been started and left unfinished for this moment to be heard as cadential. No doubt, the presence of the tritone helps. Absence of a felt downbeat is another significant factor.

Exposition

28
(Tutti)
Sn. Dr. St.
Glock
Timp. sticks (hard)
(E, C, B)
sfz
mf
p sub.
30
I →
II : C to A
II →
32
sempre f
Piu f
III : B to G
III →

Fourth step. We begin the exposition by composing the a^1 part of our proposed rondo form (*abacadaea*). According to plan, it will be eight measures long, and a tutti in contrast to the thinner-textured solo parts, *b, c, d,* and *e.* We provide rather elaborate explanation of how the meter (19/16) is to be treated, noting also the metronome mark (♪ = 180) and the constant value of the sixteenth-note. Because of the unusual signature, a beat pattern for the conductor is indicated, showing the subdivided three main pulses.

At first, we work on only the two opening measures, one part after another, striving for a degree of rhythmic counterpoint; it is evident, however, that players I-II and III-IV form two pairs. The glockenspiel is given the chief melody line, which is the row in retrograde (**R**), from E to F♯ (**R** 1–8). The timpani, already tuned to structurally significant notes in the key of E, continue to use them (E and B) along with an adjunct (C). Dynamics are largely in general agreement, but the individual lines are tailored somewhat differently.

The next two measures are composed in the same manner, but with the glockenspiel part first, since it seems to be assuming melodic primacy. After the **R**-row runs its course, we reverse it and use the original row (**O**). The line appears to want to continue, so we permit it to do so, ending with **O** 12 (the last note of **O**) at the end of a^1. We then return to m. 30, and write the other parts, two measures at a time.

Percussion I has a brief quasi-pedal in m. 30, alternate notes on the two temple blocks in mm. 31–33, and a variety of sounds as it approaches the cadence in m. 35.

Percussion III plays a sequence of m. 30 in m. 31 (or is it a varied repetition?); mm. 32–33 are similarly coupled, in an ascending rather than a descending progression, and closes (in mm. 34–35) with rather heavy "double-stops." The repeated sixteenths at the end are designed to provide a bridge to part *b.*

Percussion IV (timpani) manages to play the **R**-row between m. 30 and m. 35, a quasi-stretto in augmentation with the glockenspiel—a rather difficult part it is, too.

Fifth step. We prepare for the second section of the exposition (*b*) by drawing the bar lines, allowing three measures per system, hoping that the less complex texture will be accommodated satisfactorily. The solo spot goes to percussion III, to provide contrast from the tutti, in which the glockenspiel with its precise pitches was the melodic leader.

Accordingly, we compose a nine-measure part for the tom-toms and bass drum. Mm. 36–38 form the first small group, 37 being an almost exact repetition of 36. In m. 38, we begin to move away from repeated sixteenth, using more leaps and ties over the beats to provide a suggestion of Latin-American syncopation—without falling into any of the familiar dance patterns. (There is even a hint of the "Charleston.") Mm. 39–41 provide a second three-measure unit, in which the soloist consistently uses this type of rhythm. The closing group (mm. 42–44) is a combination of these elements, leading in m. 44 to a dissolution that is planned carefully so as to lead directly to a^2.

Having completed the solo, we return to m. 36 to write the other, accompanying parts. Percussion I is allowed to play only the tambourine and cymbal, as a part of our reduced texture and color—a short-term diet, if you will. Percussion II is largely silent, except for a few notes on the celesta, derived from the row, for a sprinkling of coloristic seasoning—this provides II with time to rest after the solo in a^1, and it will make the reentry on the glockenspiel in a^2 all the more evident and welcome. As for the timpani (in IV), we use the pitches in all three drums as we left them at the end of a^1. We are more concerned now with their rhythmic punctuation than with their pitch content. They associate with cymbal and tambourine at first, but in mm. 40–41 borrow ideas from the solo (III) and engage in imitation. Retuning in mm. 42–44 prepares us for the pitches needed in a^2. As in m. 35, we remember to write the precautionary meter change in m. 44.

Sixth step. Since part a^2 (mm. 45–51) is one measure shorter than a^1, according to our plan, we must devise the means of accomplishing this compression. Rather than simply omit one whole measure, we consider the individual lines and their needs for logical continuity. We take as our principal cue the repetition of m. 31 in 32, in percussion III. Since this repetition was, in effect, an extension, it follows that it could be omitted. We decide, then, to make our adjustments in all parts (I–IV) in these two measures.

Percussion I in mm. 45–46 is identical to mm. 28–29. In m. 47, the first two-thirds of the measure are the same as those in m. 30, but then we skip a measure and resume with the last third of m. 31.

Percussion II has a similar break in exactly the middle of m. 47.

Percussion III, as we said, simply omits the repetition observed in mm. 30–31; m. 47 is not repeated.

Percussion IV is tailored somewhat differently. Because of the use of the row, beginning with the third measure of a^1, compression in m. 47 was impractical. Inspection of the entire line revealed the presence of a varied repetition of 28 in 29. It seemed logical, therefore, to omit the very first measure. By the time we reach m. 48, the fourth measure of a^2, we are again in synchronization with a^1—m. 4 of a^2 is the same as m. 3 of a^1. From there on, we are in the home stretch. Except for the very end, m. 51, where, after the cadence on the downbeat, we try to prepare the listener for part *c*, which is in 7/8 meter and where there is more emphasis on the eighth-note than on the sixteenth. It is this endeavor that accounts for the syncopation at the end of m. 51, because the ear hears consecutive eighths with no groups. These notes lead, as a bridge, to the downbeat of m. 52.

49
piu f
dim.
dim.
dim.
III: B to G
III →
(f)
dim.
51
mf
p
mf
p
mf
dim.
p
mf
p
52
Solo
[C]
p
Sempre p
Xylo. →
f
on the metal rim, wood stick
p
(p)

Seventh step. We reduce the texture again, in part *c.* The temple blocks, which we omitted from the score in *b,* have the spotlight for eight measures, *sempre piano.* The very spare accompaniment is for percussion II and IV, who play the xylophone and only the metal rim of one of the timpani, respectively. The xylophone begins obstreperously, *forte,* but eventually is won over by the persistent calm of the temple blocks and closes softly. The idea for this procedure is derived from Beethoven's *Piano Concerto No. 4,* the slow movement, where the quiet solo piano subdues the loud demands of the orchestral strings.

The notes played by the xylophone are derived from the row, with the last two notes prolonged by repetition. They are placed so as to provide sonorities that for the most part occur when percussion I has a rest, and thus fill a rhythmic gap.

The same holds true for the timpani, except that they, like the solo, remain *piano* throughout. During the period of relatively little activity, there is opportunity for the timpani to be retuned in preparation for the return of *a.*

Part *c* dissolves, as did *b,* without cadence. M. 59 is provided with rhythmic ideas and pitches that prepare us for a^3. The dynamic level descends one notch, from *piano* to *pianissimo,* the invariable level for the next six measures.

Eighth step. In a^3, we lose an additional measure, having only six, instead of the original eight. This further compression is achieved by omitting all of the original third and fourth measures of a^1 (30–31), in all four instrumental parts—a different procedure from that used in a^2. In addition, we simplify percussion I and IV lines by omitting relatively unessential tones. Xylophone continues, replacing the glockenspiel used in *a.* And the dynamics, as just indicated, persist throughout at *pianissimo.* A case could be made for the idea that we are already using the varition principle, which we had planned to introduce in the recapitulation. If this is so, perhaps it may be justified as a foreshadowing of things to come.

60
(Tutti) a3
PP
(xylo.)
(PP)
Soft timp st.
PP
I
III
II
PP
62
III : B to G
III →
64
(III →)

Ninth step. The third contrasting section (*d*), in 3/4 meter, is again written for a reduced ensemble. The solo part is assigned to the timpani who, in the course of seven measures, play the complete row. The notes are played tremolando, with many glissandos, starting with the large drum (III), moving to II, and ending on the small drum (I). There is a fairly regular rhythmic pattern that provides two-measure groups (♩♩♩|𝅗𝅥.) with minor modifications in mm. 69 and 71.

Except for the last two measures, which are retransitional, the accompaniment consists very simply of repeated figuration in the celesta, from which we have not heard very much so far. The notes in mm. 66–68 are a scrambled arrangement of the **R**-row, 1–6; those in mm. 69–71 perform a similar service with **R** 7–12. In keeping with the nature of the instrument, the celesta remains at one level (*pp*), although the timpani rise from *pp* to *f*, then descend to *mf* and rise again to *f* at the end.

In percussion I, a suspended cymbal crescendo assists the overall rise in dynamics and tension. Tom-toms in III are the active agent in the retransition, as they predict the motive that initiates a^4.

The fermata after m. 72 helps to extend the state of suspended animation created by the tremolo crescendos and by the tom-tom sixteenths, which are left high and dry on a weak beat. It also, very practically, allows additional time for percussionist II to move from celesta to glockenspiel and prepare for the important entry in m. 73. Further, it provides a separation between structural parts that is welcome at this time, after all the previous bridges and connections.

Tenth step. In a^4, we are compressing the eight-measure a^1 into five measures. A comparison of the two reveals our procedure. Percussion IV is silent in mm. 73–74 (a judicious pause after its solo), making the canonic imitation starting in m. 75 more evident than ever. But otherwise, a^4 is nothing but the opening five measures of a^1. The last three measures are omitted. Admittedly, we made a few adjustments in the final measure of a^4 to provide a tiny connecting link to part *e*. A slight pause is indicated by the comma ('), partly for rhetorical purposes, partly for the practical reason that percussionist II needs time, once again, to move from one instrument to another. In *e*, II can begin playing as soon as ready and in position, and need not feel pressured by an inexorable beat.

Eleventh step. In *e*, the celesta finally has an opportunity to be heard in a fairly extended passage. The accompanying texture is extremely thin, mostly tremolos (in IV, I, or III), with a few metallic taps for cymbal or kettledrum's metal rim.

The six-measure solo consists of two parts, 3+3. In mm. 78–80, the melody in the treble clef is our old friend the row. The accompaniment for the first half of this three-measure phrase, in which the melody is **O** 1–6, is drawn exclusively from **O** 7–12. This procedure is reversed in the second half, where melody is **O** 7–12, accompaniment drawn from **O** 1–6.

In the second three-measure phrase or unit, the chief melodic line is now in the bass, the accompanying part above it. The melody now is based on the **R**-row, and is largely a mirror of mm. 78–80, pitch curve *and* rhythm. Again, the accompaniment for each half of the melodic phrase consists of notes drawn from the complementary half of the row—when the melody has 1–6, the accompaniment has 7–12, and vice versa.

M. 81 is both terminal, for part *e*, and preparation for a^5. The latter function is accomplished by means of the measured tremolo (in sixteenths) of indefinite length in the timpani, a long crescendo from *ppp* to *f*. This permits both the build of tension needed in a^5 and (again) needed time for percussionist II.

78
[e]
I
PPP
(PPP)
Celesta solo
II
P
III
Sn. Dr. sticks!
IV
PPP
81
poco rit.
(Sn. Dr. st.)
lunga
PPP
P sempre
poco rit.
soft timp st.
PPP
On metal rim, wood stick
(E, B, G)
ordinario!
ad lib.
(PPP)
(f)
cresc. molto

Twelfth step. The exposition in rondo form concludes with four-measure a^5, which is only half the length of a^1. The compression excludes mm. 2–5 of a^1. M. 84 is derived from m. 28, but includes much of m. 33. M. 85 restates the material of m. 34, and m. 86 is a precadential extension that repeats m. 85 almost literally. A crescendo leading to *fff* creates a climax at the cadence. M. 87 is a somewhat modified repetition of m. 35. Close examination of these two areas reveals the variation procedures used. Postcadential extension is achieved through diminuendo tremolos that lead to the development.

Development

The development section, in general outline, was described on page 191. Before getting down to realizing that plan, we decide to put the whole thing into greater focus. The section has a climax in its last part, and the preceding sections should lead up to that without being a simple straight-line crescendo. Rather, the dynamics will ebb and flow in a zigzag course similar to that used in the consecutive phrases of the exposition, where the *a* parts (8, 7, 6, 5, and 4 measures in length) alternated with contrasting *b, c, d,* and *e* (9, 8, 7, 6 measures) with the result: 8+9+7+8+6+7+5+6+4. In the development, it will be recalled, the five parts run 10+9+8+7+6, a "straight-line" plan that provides a structural counterpoint to the plan for the dynamics. A further detail pertains to the meters used: since *b, c, d,* and *e* each had a different time signature and we propose to combine the elements in the development, either we have a counterpoint of meters or we decide on one meter in which all the motivic elements will somehow be reconciled. For each of the five parts of the development, then, we decide to employ a single meter, C, 3/4, 7/8, 9/8, C, respectively.

These matters taken care of, we proceed to think about part one, mm. 88–97. Bar lines first, of course.

Thirteenth step. The ten-measure part may be subdivided. We decide on a 1+2+3+4 arrangement, using the motives *b+c+b+c* in connection with the four measure-groups. Our "1" and "2" overlap, it turns out, creating in one sense another "3." Inversion and overlap are featured in these measures, as a comparison with *b* and *c* in the exposition makes evident. The next seven measures (3+4) feature imitation.

Throughout, the texture is quite polyphonic and rather transparent. Occasional doubling helps provide contrast (see percussion I and III in mm. 94–97).

The row starts in m. 91 (xylophone), transfers to timpani in m. 92, then back to xylophone, where it ends in m. 93. A rerun is heard in the glockenspiel (mm. 94–96). In m. 97, timpani tremolos lead to part two, 3/4.

Fourteenth step. In part one of the development, we *alternated* two motives, using inversion and imitation. In part two, where we again have two motives, we have a quite different game plan. The two ideas, *d* and *e,* are used *simultaneously* (they had been presented in two separated sections).

First of all, after bar lines, we write out the *d* idea, the timpani solo from mm. 66–72, tailoring it to fit the larger dimensions of the part. Second, instead of the rather elementary celesta accompaniment used in part *d,* we work out an adaptation of *e,* which also featured the celesta. We exchange the former meter (9/8) for the new one (3/4), and simplify the part considerably, particularly in the accompanying left-hand line, but we adhere to the main contour of the lines in both right- and left-hand parts. The end is changed considerably, for several reasons: there are not enough measures to include all of the second half of the original *e,* and there is a crescendo that we wish to create, in anticipation of a raising of the tension level, hence the more active celesta part. The tones in the keyboard instrument, mm. 105–106 are taken from the left-hand line, mm. 81–83.

Percussion III is omitted altogether here. Percussion I has a repeated-tone idea that is intended to be heard as a continuation of the repeated eighths heard in m. 97, which should help to make the seam between the first and second parts of the development inconspicuous, if not invisible. The slightly premature entry of the kettledrum is another attempt to blur the border between the parts.

In keeping with our reduced instrumental color here, percussion I uses only cymbal and tambourine. The wood-blocks, the tone of which can become tiresome if they are used excessively or are overexposed, are given a deserved rest.

The rhythmic neutrality of m. 106 should help usher us into the new 7/8 meter.

Fifteenth step. The middle portion of our development (in 7/8) should combine elements of *c* and *d* in an eight-measure group. The original *c* was also eight measures, so we should be able to use most if not all of our "inheritance." What had been solo in percussion I is given now to the tom-toms (percussion III), *fff.* From part *d* we take not the solo element, but the accompaniment idea in the celesta, slightly revising the (essentially) same arpeggiated harmony. The other players have secondary material, but it should be observed that we have rather close canonic imitation in mm. 111–112. Deliberate contrast between *fff* and *pp* puts the accented rhythms in bold relief. M. 114 is a dissolution preparing for and leading to the 9/8 part that follows.

Sixteenth step. The fourth part of our development section will attempt to combine *three* elements, namely *b, c,* and *e,* in contrast to parts 1–3, which contained only two each. The previous part (in 7/8) included *c* elements, which now provide a degree of connection and continuity.

Turning first to our treatment of *c,* we decide to restore this material to the temple blocks (see mm. 52ff), rather than continue or repeat the idea in the tom-toms (see mm. 107ff). It is adjusted from 7/8 to 9/8 by the addition of eighth-note rests. Furthermore, we use only the first four measures of *c* (52–55) in the following sequence, considering m. 52 as *1,* m. 53 as *2,* etc.: *1-2-3-4-3-2-1.* In other "language," our seven measures in 9/8 are in an arch (or mirror) form. This is a retrograde use of measures as such, but not rhythmic retrograde *within* the measures. Except for the last measure (121) the materials tend to lie in the latter part of each measure-unit.

We decide, further, to repeat the same kind of retrograde or mirror procedure in the first four measures of *b,* and similarly to use the original instrumentation, tom-toms (see mm. 36ff). The measures drawn on are (in order) 36-37-38-39-38-37-36. In mm. 115–121, 118 is the pivot, in both percussion I and III.

We give the *e* materials to percussion II. We do not use the arch form of the two lines already written, but, instead, write two three-measure units with a one-measure caesura in the middle (3+1+3). The first "3," in the celesta, is derived from the chief melody notes of the solo in mm. 78–80; the second "3" is played by the glockenspiel, for contrast, and is derived in similar fashion from mm. 81–83.

Timpani (percussion IV) provide a "free" or new part, using notes removed from F and E (first and last notes of the row), with mm. 121–122 providing a slightly varied repetition of mm. 118–119. The dotted eighths and sixteenths make this part sound more like 3/4 than 9/8, thus adding to the tension.

Dynamics play an important role in the structure, sometimes providing sharp contrast, elsewhere crescendos and diminuendos, all within a basic framework of *p-f-p.* Sixteenths at the end lead directly to the fifth (and last) part of the development.

Seventeenth step. The final portion of the development utilizes material from all parts of the exposition except *a.* It should provide a climax to the work as a whole and leads, as retransition, to the recapitulation. We have given ourselves only six measures (122–127) in which to accomplish several important tasks.

Let us proceed by writing the *b, c, d,* and *e* elements in turn. The first of these we retain in the tom-toms, which are best able to project its character. The line is thus a slightly varied repetition of what we heard in mm. 115–121, but consistently loud, from m. 123. M. 122 is a tiny bridge leading into the main body of the phrase, allowing for separation of structural parts and for tuning (in timpani) and changing position (glockenspiel to xylophone). We use arch form: *12321* (see *sixteenth step,* paragraph 2).

As for *c,* it appears in mm. 115ff in percussion I much as it did originally, except for the tailoring needed for the meter. We again use arch form, but now *12321,* not *1234321.*

The *d* idea, like *b,* is rather idiomatic and does not lend itself too well to instrumental change. And there is little point in having timpani imitate tom-toms, which they *could* do but to no great advantage. So we leave *d* in the timpani (percussion IV), where it appears *ff* without the tremolos. The force of the notes is considerably greater when they are played singly rather than tremolando, and we *are* trying to build a climax—sufficient reason for that alteration.

And, finally, *e* appears, but not in the celesta, where it would be almost inaudible given the context. The solo material is treated somewhat as in mm. 115–121, in quasi-diminution and arpeggiated, that is to say. The xylophone has the first three measures, 123–125; the glockenspiel is given the balance (126–127).

This is the only part of the development that presents simultaneous treatment of *four* previously stated ideas. That, plus the *ff*-crescendo, should create our planned climax. To aid the sense of sustained intensity, we terminate the development with a fermata, following a brief ritardando. The lack of a decisive downbeat and the conflicting rhythms should make it clear that we are not yet at the very end.

Eighteenth step. Before starting the next large section, the recapitulation, we should review all the music composed up to this point, to assess exactly how our plan is working out and what adjustments may be needed.

From the writer's vantage point, it seems evident that there has been a slight tendency toward "busy-ness," and we should therefore seek all suitable means of reducing the amount of simultaneous activity. We will aspire to more transparent textures, less counterpoint, more lightly scored homophony. Fortunately, our plans envisaged the return of the solo sections *b, c, d,* and *e,* which are already thin and which probably do not need to be varied.

Our first subdivision, the opening tutti (mm. 128–135), corresponds in length and substance to the initial tutti of the exposition, mm. 28–35. Since we have just reached the climax of the movement, we permit the opening *a* to sustain the intensity and dynamic level achieved at the end of the development.[2]

We planned it as a variation, and we look for the best way to accomplish this in the light of our determination to sustain tension a bit longer. Our solution is to provide percussion II and III with canonic imitation, thickening the parts from single to double lines throughout most of the eight measures. In the glockenspiel, this turns out to be a canon at the octave after one measure. In the tom-toms, however, it is a very close canon after three eights and within the measure only.

2. This statement is not really a contradiction of the plan outlined in the previous paragraph regarding reduction of tension. It should be observed as a *short*-term departure from the still-valid principle intended for the *long*-term design of the recapitulation. The net result is a structural elision that helps to connect development and recapitulation.

An additional variation may be discerned in the dynamics, which abruptly alternate between *ff* and *p*, instead of ranging from *f* to *p* with numerous crescendos and diminuendos. These apparently erratic changes assist the maintenance of tension. Only in the last two measures do we find a diminuendo, *ff* to *mf*, a direct lead to the reduced tension and dynamics of the next part, *b*.

Recapitulation

132
ff sub.
p
ff
ff sub.
p sub.
ff sub.
p
III : B to G
III →
(ff)
p
134
(♪=♪)
(ff)
mf
ff
f
mf
ff
mf
(III)
ff
f
p
136
b
PP
mf
sec
sec
p
solo
(Hard timp. st.)
5
5
p
mf
p
ordinario!
sec
sec
sec
p

139
(SHAKE)
(thumb)
(P)
mf
P
Celesta
mf
mf
P
mf
P
mf
sec
mf
P
mf
142
(heel)
mf
sfz
(sn. Dr. st.)
P
(celesta)
mf
(Xylo.→)
5
f mf
P non. cresc.
mf sub.
P
III
II
I
P
mf
P
PP
145
Solo [C]
P
f sub.
xylo.
f
(f)
wood stick on metal rim [sn. Dr. st.]
P
(P)
f

Nineteenth step. The *b* portion presents no problems. It satisfies the need for reduced tensions and a more transparent texture. It remains then only for the music of mm. 36–44 to be copied in mm. 136–144.

Twentieth step. Our altered rondo form omits the *a* between *b* and *c* in the recapitulation. We may proceed with *c* without further ado. Happily, we may continue the reduced texture. A few increases in dynamics help achieve contrast and dramatic suspense. Except for connections at the beginning and the end, there are no points that need alteration. The eight-measure *c,* like the nine-measure *b,* retains its original length and its characteristic meter.

Twenty-first step. Another varied restatement of *a* forms the very center of the recapitulation. We predetermined its length, seven measures, the same as that of a^2, but for several reasons prefer to base the present return of *a* on a^3, which had only six measures. This does not create any problem, but rather provides (in m. 159) an opportunity to have a welcome extra-length transition to *d*.

The chief changes are in the figuration of the xylophone part (more sixteenths now) and in the considerable use of glissando for both xylophone and timpani. The two types of glissando (diatonic, or "white key," in the xylophone, chromatic in the timpani) provide contrasts themselves. Timpani, in addition, have glissandos that are sometimes slurred and sometimes not. The former are played with a single stroke of the drumstick, whereas the latter involve a stroke at the end as well as at the beginning of the slide.[3]

Twenty-second step. The *d* section follows (mm. 160–166). It corresponds in substance and length to the original *d* and differs only in very minor detail. There is no need for transition to the *e* section that follows, except for a bit of adjustment in the celesta arpeggio in m. 166 so that the line leads directly to the note (F) that is needed for the start of *e*. By happy coincidence, the instrumentation of parts *d* and *e* is much the same, making the two parts seem almost as one.

3. Glissandos played tremolando are still another type.

Tutti [a var. 2]
153
(Xylo.)
(l.h.) (r.h.)
Gliss
(r.h.)(l.h.)
Gliss
(Hard timp st.)
I Gliss.
III
II
I
III II
Gliss.
III: B to G
156
sfz
l.h.
r.h.
Gliss
sfz
(f)
mf
III→ Gliss.
Gliss.
ff
mf
159
pp
Celesta→
p legato
(III)→ Solo
p
mf
p

Twenty-third step. The six-measure *e* part is more a variation of the original *e* (mm. 78–83) than an exact restatement of it. We retain measure-for-measure correspondence, but exchange small leaps for wide ones by octave displacement. The texture is primarily two-voiced, with occasional thickening to three lines. The extremely light accompaniment is even more limited than before. Percussion I takes a rest, while III and IV are allotted but a few taps. The tom-tom tremolo in m. 172 is simply an anticipation of m. 173. It helps bridge the gap while percussionist II changes from celesta to xylophone. The fermata should last only long enough to provide time for that maneuver.[4]

The low level of the dynamics is part of a larger design that is gradually getting into focus. We envisage a large diminuendo to the very end of the recapitulation, with corresponding reduction of tension as close to zero as possible without permitting the momentum to cease altogether. This is designed partly to balance the exposition and the development, both of which ended *ff*, and also to prepare for the coda which we are beginning to see as a quite effective, long, and gradual crescendo to the end. Percussion instruments tend to be identified in most minds as the noise-making apparatus of the orchestra, as the brasses are associated with loud volume. The more tender and lyrical aspects of the percussion department are largely unexplored, and if we poke about in that direction, it is partly to uncover some new aesthetic possibilities for these instruments, for so long a time relatively neglected and limited as adjuncts to others. Add the percussion department to the list of minority groups seeking equal status and opportunity!

4. Stravinsky uses the same procedure with the snare drum during the brief scene changes in his ballet *Petrouchka*.

167
[e]
I
II
Solo [Celesta]
p
III, IV
Perc. III Wood st. [or Sn. Dr. st.]
pp
(Perc. IV→)
170
(♪=♪)
(19/16)
(Xylo→)
Timp Wood stick on metal rim
pp
(Perc. III→) (sn. Dr. st.)
ad lib.
ppp
Tutti [a Var. 3] (♪=♪)
173
(heel)
ppp sempre
xylo.
ppp sempre
III
ppp sempre
IV
wood sticks on metal rim
ppp

Coda

Twenty-fourth step. With mm. 173–178, we reach the final variant restatement of *a* and the end of the recapitulation. Ending the section quietly, we reduce the volume to *ppp,* and end as close as possible to "absolute zero" (*quasi niente,* "almost nothing"). The substance of *a* here is related most closely to a^3 of the exposition, which was the same length. A few modifications, including octave displacements, may be observed. Also, the xylophone part is largely tremolando rather than consisting of single strokes or sixteenths. Tom-toms are of like mind. Only in percussion I and IV do we find a few almost-inaudible metallic taps. The suspended cymbal played with soft timpani sticks is capable of playing the reduction to near-nothingness better than almost any other percussion instrument, and it leads to the coda without there being any interruption, while almost all sense of meter or beat has vanished.

Twenty-fifth step. We begin our twenty-seven-measure, three-section coda (10+9+8) with a group that borrows materials from *b* and *d,* according to our stated plan. Mindful of the fact that a coda is often a second development, we try to think of procedures we have not used in the development section. Of course, *b* and *d* did not appear in counterpoint except in the final portion of the development, where *everything* except *a* made an appearance. Rather than use all or most of *b* and *d,* we shall attempt to use fragments—a classic procedure—and both sequence and imitation such as to suggest double counterpoint. Texture will remain rather thin, and dynamics low, so that our long-range crescendo and increase of tension can be properly controlled.

For meter, we adopt C, which had been used in part *b.* We increase the tempo slightly, from 180 to 200, to assist the growing rise in tension, another classic device.

The first three measures of the coda (mm. 179–181) are *ppp,* mysterious in effect, very transparent in texture. Motivic derivations from part *b* (m. 36) are much in evidence at first, followed by the jazzy rhythmic idea from m. 39. From part *d,* we have the row, in the timpani, but now in retrograde rather than in the original sequence, with a supplemental repetition of the first four notes (E-D♯-A-B♭) in the xylophone, which results in a rare case of parallel octaves.

The ensuing three measures (182–184) reveal our plan to have a gradual thickening of texture and consequent very slow increase of tension. In m. 182, the xylophone has the row from *d,* tom-toms the rhythm from *b* (m. 36). Timpani continue the **R**-row. In m. 183, there is canonic imitation between percussion I and III. The **O**-row (7–12) appears in the glockenspiel, mm. 183–184, completing the row in a modified sequence of the notes in m. 182. Also in m. 184, in the timpani, is the use of backtracking in the row, where **R** 11 is followed by **R** 7 instead of the expected **R** 12, following which we continue to 11, this time going on to 12 at the cadence, in m. 188.

We repeat mm. 182–184 in mm. 184–186 with rhythmic displacement of the accents. Another brief fling at canonic imitation appears between percussion II and III in mm. 185–186, although it cannot be precise, of course, because the *dux* involves pitched sounds whereas the *comes* only *suggests* the rising pitch line. The two last measures are rather complex in the rhythmic counterpoint department, thanks to the half-note triplets in the xylophone, which seems to be trying to steal the show with its "double-stops" and crescendo to *forte.* Sanity is preserved in percussion III, fortunately, as we observe the brief preparation for the second part of the coda by virtue of the motive that is introduced at the end of m. 188.

Twenty-sixth step. Moving on to part two of the coda, we have nine measures in 9/8, which can be adapted to the 7/8 of part *c*.

We continue the gradual growth in intensity through a thickening of texture and by raising the dynamic level from *p* to *f*. Motives from *c* and *e* appear in this part, with considerable use of contrapuntal techniques. The tom-toms, beginning at m. 189, play an adaptation of the celesta melody from part *e* (mm. 78ff) while fragments of *c* are heard in the other parts. The use of the metal rim in the timpani, and the rhythm, too, is from *c*. Then, as if in canonic imitation with the tom-toms, the celesta begins a four-measure passage in m. 191 in which the **O**-row and the **R**-row appear simultaneously with identical rhythms. The contrary motion suggests to the listener that the row is being used with its inversion, a device that may be thought of as similar to the *trompe l'oeil* technique in architecture, where a painted column tempts the eye to believe that the structural column continues beyond the point where it ends in fact.

At m. 192, tom-toms continue their adaptation (a sort of instrumental "translation") of the celesta melody from m. 81. The celesta uses double counterpoint in the repetition of m. 193 in 194, which marks the end of the solo line in part *e*: we are again using whole melodies, as well as fragments, from previous sections.

Although we are still in part two, there is need for an unmistakable retransition to the third part of the coda, which is based upon *a*. It occurs to us to borrow material from the very end of the slow introduction, which has not otherwise been heard from. And so we do that, altering it to fit the new situation. An accelerando leads to a further change of tempo. After allowing time for percussionist II to move from celesta to glockenspiel, we anticipate *a* motivically in percussion II and III, while I builds up a nice, frothy crescendo on the suspended cymbal, and IV gets regular sticks ready for use.

197 [sempre col legno]
(♪=♪) Tutti [a] Ancora più mosso [♪=228 or ♩.=76]
Glock.
ordinario!
I
II
III
199
simile
201

Twenty-seventh step. The thrill of writing the last bar lines and the double bar at the end is exceeded only by the writing of the last few notes. And so we start the final part of the coda.

In eight measures, we should provide a real sense of conclusion as well as a further return of *a,* which, however, will receive here still another treatment as a variation.

The first of these tasks requires the most thought; the others will almost take care of themselves. The timpani, with their precise tunings, can provide a kind of settling down that the others can do only by a sustained tremolo or exact repetition. We set up, therefore, a quasi-ostinato for the timpani, using all three drums, tuned to E, C, and B. E is one of the two tones that frame our row, the other being F. The B thus serves as V-of-E. The F we decide to save for the very end, where the presumed tonic (E) suddenly becomes the leading tone of F. Or is that F a "Neapolitan" (♭II) of E? The "unanswered question" is more a reminiscence of Richard Strauss's *Also Sprach Zarathustra,* which ends ambiguously in C or B major, than it is of Charles Ives's short piece (*The Unanswered Question*), whose ambiguities go far beyond the matter of tonality.

But to return to the timpani—our ostinato figure includes the idea of ever-increasing note values, up to the end, where we slip chromatically from B down the tritone to F.

To sustain intensity, we maintain *ff* up to the *fff* conclusion. A few added notes, leaps, octave doublings, etc., should raise a few pulses, if not the roof. The faster tempo of the final tutti should add further zest. Accents, particularly to distinguish from are to be carefully observed in performance.

Twenty-eighth step. As always: we carefully review the manuscript for errors and possible revision; then we copy the parts. And need we mention the rehearsals and the performance?

Twenty-ninth step. In conclusion, we should not neglect the opportunity to attempt an objective evaluation of the work. How well does it "come off" as music? Does it please others, or is it just a tonal sand castle that is fun for the maker but of little more than patronizing interest to would-be well-wishers masquerading as friends? Are there unsatisfactory elements that can be altered? If so, can the alterations be made without changing the entire character of the piece? Is there too much of something? Too little? Did we omit something that still can be added, or is something in need of surgical removal? And so forth and so on.

The author, not having heard the work, which was written at the same time as these words, does not have answers to those questions, but he intends to ask them in due course. They are spelled out here not so much for his benefit as for the reader's, because it is hoped that student composers will penetratingly evaluate *themselves* as they write one work after another and not succumb to excesses of self-congratulation, an exercise in which they are sure to be aided and abetted by doting family and friends. On the other hand, one should guard against an excess of negative self-criticism, which may inhibit the flow of vital creative juices. Somewhere between the two is the golden mean of objectivity, not coldly calculating, but warmly appreciative of the fact that there is likely to be some value in every created work, and that no seriously wrought work of art is all bad. Or even perfect—unless it is the product of genius.

Exercise 14.1 *Make a fairly detailed preliminary draft of precompositional assumptions for a work of fairly lengthy proportions, in one movement. Include as many parameters as possible, adding others later if necessary. This should be sufficiently detailed so that a composition teacher can examine it and make suggestions regarding alterations, or give you the "green light" to go ahead.*

Examine each step along the way, and evaluate it before you take the next one. Describe in essay form your thoughts and the bases for your decisions. You may use the format of this chapter as a model. The music should be prepared for the performers and played for what one hopes is a sympathetic audience. Encourage performers and knowledgeable listeners to comment on their reactions, remembering at the same time that they may tell you more about themselves than about your music!

Exercise 14.2 *Write a work of several movements, displaying appropriate unity and contrast. You may wish to review the models mentioned in* KMF, *Chapter 26, and of course music libraries are repositories of innumerable scores that await your inspection and analysis. You may or may not duplicate their successes, or equal their accomplishments, but the resultant stimulation from such exposure is sure to have a beneficial effect on your own creative thought.*

References

Apel, Willi (ed.), *Harvard Dictionary of Music,* Harvard University Press, 1944, the article "Composition" (E. B. Hill). (The third section lists some standard texts.)

Attwood, Thomas, *Theorie- und Kompositionsstudien bei Mozart* (Theory and Composition Studies with W. A. Mozart), in *Neue Ausgabe sämtlicher Werke,* Serie X, Supplement, Werkgruppe 30, Bärenreiter, Kassel, 1965. (Harmony and counterpoint are studied on pages 3–166, composition on pages 167–254. Attwood's writing is shown in black, Mozart's in red.)

Basart, Ann P., *Serial Music: A Classified Bibliography of Writings on Twelve-Tone and Electronic Music.* University of California Press, 1961 (Compositional techniques are listed in entries 119–175, 272–283, 380–394, and 583–586.)

Chavez, Carlos, *Toward a New Music,* W. W. Norton, 1937. (Chapters on film music, radio, and other electronic applications.)

Cooper, Grosvenor, and Leonard B. Meyer, *The Rhythmic Structure of Music,* University of Chicago Press, 1960.

Cooper, Paul, *Perspectives in Music Theory,* Dodd, Mead, 1973. (Chapters 28–30 review twentieth-century techniques and styles.)

Copland, Aaron, *Our New Music,* Whittlesey House (McGraw-Hill), 1941.

Cowell, Henry, *New Musical Resources,* A. A. Knopf, 1930.

Dallin, Leon, *Techniques of Twentieth Century Composition,* Wm. C. Brown, 1957. (Text includes examples and assignments.)

Eschman, Karl, *Changing Forms in Modern Music,* E. C. Schirmer, 1945.

Forte, Allen, *The Structure of Atonal Music,* Yale University Press, 1973. (Elaborates on set theory, with illustrations from ten composers.)

Graf, Max, *From Beethoven to Shostakovich: The Psychology of the Composing Process,* Philosophical Library, 1947.

Graves, William L., Jr., *Twentieth Century Fugue,* Catholic University of America Press, 1962.

Hindemith, Paul, *The Craft of Musical Composition,* Associated Music Publishers, 1941. Translated by Otto Ortmann. (Volume 1, Theory; Volume 2, Exercises in two-part writing.)

Hitchcock, H. Wiley, *Music in the United States: A Historical Introduction,* Prentice-Hall, 1969. (Part 3 treats the years after 1920.)

Indy, Vincent d', *Cours de composition musicale,* A. Durand, Paris, 1903, 1909, 1933. (A multi-volumed review of the history of musical composition in the western world.)

Karkoschka, Erhard, *Notation in New Music,* Universal Edition, 1972. Translated by Ruth Koenig. (A comprehensive and well-illustrated survey.)

Lenormand, René, *A Study of Twentieth Century Harmony*, Joseph Williams, (London), 1915. Translated by Herbert Antcliffe. (Covers French music of the century up to 1914.)

Lowinsky, Edward E., *Tonality and Atonality in Sixteenth-Century Music,* University of California Press, 1961. (Chapter 16 concerns "Floating Tonality and Atonality in Sixteenth-Century Music.")

Messiaen, Olivier, *The Technique of My Musical Language,* Alphonse Leduc (Paris), 1956. Translated by John Satterfield.

Perle, George, *Serial Composition and Atonality,* University of California Press, 1962. (Largely a description of the compositional techniques of Schoenberg, Berg, and Webern, with a few references to Babbitt, Bartók, Krenek, Messiaen, and Stravinsky.)

Persichetti, Vincent, *Twentieth-century Harmony,* W. W. Norton, 1961. (Most of the illustrations are by the author. Each chapter includes suggested exercises and concludes with suggestions of works to be examined.)

Schillinger, Joseph, *The Schillinger System of Musical Composition,* Carl Fischer, 1946. (See also the review of this book by Nicolas Slonimsky, *Musical Quarterly,* July, 1946.

Schoenberg, Arnold, *Harmonielehre* (Theory of Harmony), Faber and Faber, (London), 1978; (in the U.S.A., University of California Press). Translated by Roy E. Carter. (This is a new translation of the original [Vienna, 1911]; an earlier translation, by Robert Adams [Philosophical Library, 1948], is incomplete.)

———, *Models for Beginners in Composition,* G. Schirmer, 1942. (A text based upon Schoenberg's experience as teacher, at U.C.L.A.)

———, *Structural Functions of Harmony,* W. W. Norton, 1954. Edited by Humphrey Searle. (Largely concerned with eighteenth- and nineteenth-century compositional processes, and the application of harmony to form.)

Searle, Humphrey, *Twentieth Century Counterpoint,* Williams and Norgate (London), (Reprinted 1979 by Hyperion Press [Encore Music ed.].)

Slonimsky, Nicolas, *Thesaurus of Scales and Musical Patterns,* Coleman-Ross, 1946.

Smith Brindle, Reginald, *Serial Composition,* Oxford University Press, 1966. (Lucid text with illustrations and exercises.)

Toch, Ernst, *The Shaping Forces in Music,* Criterion, 1958.

Vinton, John (Editor), *Dictionary of Contemporary Music,* E. P. Dutton, 1971. (See, *inter alia,* the articles on Electronic music: Notation (Brian Fennelly); Indeterminancy (Barney Childs); Jazz (Frank Tirro); Notation (Kurt Stone); Performance, and Rhythm (both by Frederick Rzewski); Serialism (Ernst Krenek); and Theory (Allen Forte). The last-named includes an extensive bibliography.)

Index

Numbers in italics denote pages with musical illustrations.